LONGMAN
PRONUNCIATION DICTIONARY
STUDY GUIDE
Clare Fletcher

LONGMAN
PRONUNCIATION DICTIONARY
STUDY GUIDE

Clare Fletcher

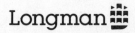

Longman Group UK Limited
Longman House, Burnt Mill, Harlow,
Essex CM20 2JE, England
and Associated Companies throughout the world.

© Longman Group UK Limited 1990

ISBN 0 582 05386 2

Second impression 1992

Set in Monophoto Century Schoolbook

Produced by Longman Singapore Publishers Pte Ltd
Printed in Singapore

CONTENTS

Introduction

Part A: Pronunciations and variants

1. Characters used in phonemic transcription   ex.1–8

2. What pronunciations are given: the layout of entries   ex.9–11

3. Alternative pronunciations

    DIAGNOSTIC EXERCISE   ex.12
    ALTERNATIVES AT THE BEGINNING OF A WORD   ex.13
    ALTERNATIVES AT THE END OF A WORD   ex.14
    ALTERNATIVES IN THE MIDDLE OF A WORD   ex.15
    COMBINATIONS OF ALTERNATIVES   ex.16
    ALTERNATIVE PRONUNCIATIONS INVOLVING THE SYMBOL ▪   ex.17
    QUIZ ON ALTERNATIVE PRONUNCIATIONS   ex.18

4. Inflected and derived words   ex.19–20

    APPLICATION EXERCISES ON LAYOUT OF ENTRIES,
      ALTERNATIVE PRONUNCIATIONS, INFLECTIONS AND
      DERIVED FORMS   ex.21–22

5. Optional sounds

    SOUNDS SHOWN IN ITALICS: ELISION   ex.23–26
    SOUNDS SHOWN BY RAISED LETTERS: INSERTION   ex.27
    CONVERSATION FOR STUDY: OPTIONAL SOUNDS   ex.28

6. Syllabic consonants   ex.29–31

7. Compression

    COMPRESSION INVOLVING A CONSONANT   ex.32–35
    COMPRESSION INVOLVING A VOWEL   ex.36–37
    CONVERSATION FOR STUDY: SYLLABIC CONSONANTS AND   ex.38
      COMPRESSION

Part B: Stress in words and phrases

8. Pairs of words with different stress ex.39–43

9. Stress marking

 PRIMARY STRESS ex.44–45
 SECONDARY AND PRIMARY STRESS ex.46–47
 TERTIARY STRESS ex.48–50
 MIXED PATTERNS ex.51–53

10. Stress shift ex.54–58

11. Compounds and phrases ex.59–63

12. Alternative pronunciations with different stress ex.64–66

13. Suffixes ex.67–69

Part C: Aspects of pronunciation in the dictionary

14. American pronunciation

 SIX DIFFERENCES BETWEEN BRITISH AND AMERICAN ex.70–75
  ENGLISH
 QUIZZES ON AMERICAN PRONUNCIATION ex.76–77
 TEXT FOR STUDY: AMERICAN PRONUNCIATION ex.78

15. Homophones ex.79

16. Abbreviations ex.80

17. Names of people and places ex.81

18. Assimilation ex.82–83

 TEXT FOR STUDY: ASSIMILATION ex.84

19. Pronunciations derived by rule ex.85

20. Incorrect pronunciations ex.86

21. Combining forms ex.87–88

Key to Exercises

INTRODUCTION

This study guide enables readers to make the best use of the
Longman Pronunciation Dictionary. The dictionary and study
guide together are a powerful aid to the study of English
pronunciation.

WHAT THE STUDY GUIDE CONTAINS

- Discussion of features of English pronunciation shown in the
  dictionary and explanation of the conventions used to show
  them.
- Exercises to develop effective use of the dictionary.
- Cross-references to relevant material in the dictionary's
  introduction and notes.
- Diagnostic exercises in the early sections to enable you to
  assess your proficiency and select appropriate material.
- Explicit statements of aims to show the purpose of each
  exercise.
- A key at the back of the book for checking the answers to
  exercises, where these are not immediately obvious from the
  dictionary.

The **cassette** provides three types of material:
- Illustration of pronunciations you see in the book and
  dictionary.
- Exercises.
- A means of checking your answers to certain exercises.

HOW TO USE THE STUDY GUIDE

You can work through the guide from beginning to end, or you
can plan your own programme to meet your needs.

Planning a programme
- Look at the Contents List.
- Use the diagnostic exercises in the early sections.
- Look at the aims of sections and of specific exercises.
- Select the sections and exercises which are useful for you.

Using the commentary and exercises

- It is always helpful to *say* the pronunciations you are reading, to make them clear and to fix them in your memory. This may not be possible, for example if you are working in a library. But if you are working by yourself, or with others also using the study guide, make a habit of saying the pronunciations.
- Always look up pronunciations in the dictionary when you are told to do so. In some exercises, the words to look up begin with the same letter, to speed up the search.
- Some exercises involve transcription; you can get further practice by transcribing any of the dialogues and texts in the book and cassette, and these are transcribed in the key at the back of the book.
- Look up cross-references to the introduction or notes in the dictionary, if you want to take a point further.

RP	Gen Am	Consonants		RP	Gen Am	Vowels	
•	•	p	pen, copy, happen	•	•	ɪ	kit, bid, hymn
•	•	b	back, bubble, job	•	•	e	dress, bed
•	•	t	tea, tight, button	•	•	æ	trap, bad
•		ţ	city, better	•		ɒ	lot, odd, wash
•	•	d	day, ladder, odd	•	•	ʌ	strut, bud, love
•	•	k	key, cock, school	•	•	ʊ	foot, good, put
•	•	g	get, giggle, ghost				
				•	•	iː	fleece, sea, machine
•	•	tʃ	church, match, nature	•	•	eɪ	face, day, steak
•	•	dʒ	judge, age, soldier	•	•	aɪ	price, high, try
				•	•	ɔɪ	choice, boy
•	•	f	fat, coffee, rough, physics				
•	•	v	view, heavy, move	•	•	uː	goose, two, blue
•	•	θ	thing, author, path	•		əʊ	goat, show, no
•	•	ð	this, other, smooth		•	oʊ	goat, show, no
•	•	s	soon, cease, sister		•	ɒʊ	variant in cold
•	•	z	zero, zone, roses, buzz	•	•	aʊ	mouth, now
•	•	ʃ	ship, sure, station	•		ɪə	near, here, serious
•	•	ʒ	pleasure, vision	•		eə	square, fair, various
•	•	h	hot, whole, behind	•	•	ɑː	start, father
					•	ɑː	lot, odd
•	•	m	more, hammer, sum		•	ɒː	thought, law
•	•	n	nice, know, funny, sun	•		ɔː	thought, law
•	•	ŋ	ring, long, thanks, sung	•	•	ɔː	north, war
					•	oː	variant in force, four
•	•	l	light, valley, feel	•		ʊə	cure, poor, jury
•	•	r	right, sorry, arrange	•		ɜː	nurse, stir
					•	ɝː	nurse, stir, courage
•	•	j	yet, use, beauty				
•	•	w	wet, one, when, queen	•	•	i	happy, radiation, glorious
				•	•	ə	about, comma, common
In foreign words only:				•	•	u	influence, situation, annual
•	•	x	loch, chutzpah	•	•	ɪ	intend, basic
•		ɬ	Llanelli, Hluhluwe	•		ʊ	stimulus, educate

In foreign words only:

RP	Gen Am		
•		ɒ̃	grand prix, chanson
•	•	ɑ̃ː	grand prix, chanson
•		ɔ̃ː	chanson
•	•	æ̃	vingt-et-un
•		ɛ̃ː	vingt-et-un

A PRONUNCIATION AND VARIANTS

1 Characters used in phonemic transcription

The chart on the previous page shows the characters which are used to transcribe pronunciations in the dictionary. The sounds and key words are recorded on the cassette, followed by the vowel sounds in sequence.

Within words, syllable boundaries are shown by spaces
e.g. ˌɪn dɪ 'pend ənt

EXERCISE 1

DIAGNOSTIC EXERCISE IN READING STRAIGHTFORWARD PHONEMIC TRANSCRIPTIONS QUICKLY AND ACCURATELY.

Time yourself as you do this exercise.
For each of the words a–j below, find the correct phonemic transcription in the list on the right. Write its number next to the word. The first one is done for you.

a. **await** 5 ....

b. **billow** ....

c. **chose** ....

d. **creature** ....

e. **drudge** ....

f. **hurt** ....

g. **jet** ....

h. **orange** ....

i. **sergeant** ....

j. **wrecked** ....

1. krɪ 'eɪt ə
2. jet
3. 'ɒ rɪndʒ
4. tʃəʊz
5. ə 'weɪt
6. dʒet
7. bɪ 'ləʊ
8. 'sɜːdʒ ən
9. ə 'reɪndʒ
10. hɑːt
11. drʌg
12. 'bɪl əʊ
13. rekt
14. 'æv ɪd
15. tʃɔɪs
16. 'sɑːdʒ ənt
17. 'kriːtʃ ə
18. drʌdʒ
19. 'retʃ ɪd
20. hɜːt

starting time:
....
finishing time:
....
time taken:
....

1

KEY

Check your answers to exercise 1 with the key at the back of the book.

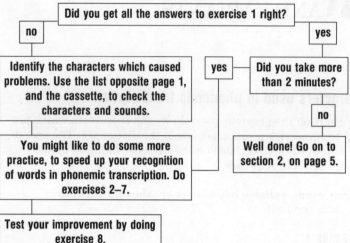

EXERCISES 2–8
AIM: TO PRACTISE RECOGNISING AND PRODUCING STRAIGHTFORWARD PHONEMIC TRANSCRIPTIONS.

EXERCISE 2

KEY

Look back at the transcriptions in exercise 1. Write the words represented by the ten transcriptions which did not match a–j.

EXERCISE 3

Which word does each of the transcriptions below represent? Circle the correct word. Work as quickly as you can. The first one is done for you.

		A	B
1.	aɪs	eyes	(ice)
2.	'æŋkəl	ankle	uncle
3.	səʊl	soil	soul
4.	briːð	breathe	breath
5.	ə'vɔɪd	avoid	evade
6.	θɪŋ	thin	thing
7.	'pəʊz ɪz	possess	poses
8.	vaɪn	vein	vine
9.	'luːv ə	louvre	lover
10.	'fiːl ɪŋz	fillings	feelings

KEY

You can check your answers in the key and on the cassette.

EXERCISE 4

KEY Look back at the pairs of words given in exercise 3. For each pair, transcribe the one not transcribed on the left.

EXERCISE 5

Read the transcriptions below, and then listen to the eight words on the cassette. For each word, write the letter of the correct transcription beside the corresponding number. The first one is KEY done for you.

a. 'leð ə   e. 'kætʃ ə   i. liːd ə   m. 'kɒŋ kɔːd
b. 'wɒʃ ɪŋ   f. luːs   j. eɪdʒ   n. ə'laɪv
c. kæ 'ʃɪə   g. 'wɒtʃ ɪŋ   k. 'ɒl ɪv   o. luːz
d. 'leʒ ə   h. edʒ   l. 'kɒŋ kəd   p. 'ledʒ ə

1. ..i.. 2. .... 3. .... 4. .... 5. .... 6. .... 7. .... 8. ....

EXERCISE 6

KEY Look back at transcriptions a–p in exercise 5. Write the eight words shown which were not given on the cassette.
You can check your answers in the key and on the cassette.

EXERCISE 7

In the following pairs of words, is the first syllable the same (S) or different (D)? Use the dictionary to check. The first two are KEY done for you.

1 **worthy**	**worried**	D		7. **majestic**	**magician**	....
2. **feral**	**ferrous**	S		8. **patient**	**patio**	....
3. **dynasty**	**dynamite**	....		9. **southeast**	**southern**	....
4. **variegated**	**various**	....		10. **period**	**pierrot**	....
5. **vagary**	**vagabond**	....		11. **nutrient**	**nutmeg**	....
6. **vicissitude**	**vicar**	....		12. **foreign**	**forecast**	....

EXERCISE 8

Time yourself as you do this exercise.
For each of the words a–j below, find the correct phonemic transcription in the list on the right. Write its letter next to the word. The first one is done for you.

a. **season** !ⁱ⁹

b. **wordy** ....

c. **foreman** ....

d. **neuter** ....

e. **phonetic** ....

f. **sinner** ....

g. **shield** ....

h. **organ** ....

i. **please** ....

j. **jeer** ....

1. 'sɪŋ ə
2. fə 'net ɪk
3. ə 'gen
4. 'fɔː mən
5. 'nʌt ə
6. ʃiːld
7. jɪə
8. fə 'næt ɪk
9. 'sɪn ə
10. 'pleʒ ə
11. 'njuːt ə
12. 'wɜːd i
13. 'siːz ɪŋ
14. dʒɪə
15. pliːz
16. siːld
17. 'ɔːg ən
18. 'fɔː neɪm
19. 'siːz ən
20. 'wɜːð i

starting time:

....

finishing time:

....

time taken:

....

KEY

Check your answers with the key. Did you do better than in exercise 1? Were you more accurate and/or quicker?

2 What pronunciations are given: the layout of entries

For every word the dictionary gives a main pronunciation. This is highlighted in blue. If the American pronunciation is different, it is given, following the symbol ‖, and also highlighted in blue. If no separate American pronunciation is given, this means that the word has the same pronunciation in British and American English.

| match mætʃ |

| dot, Dot dɒt‖ dɑːt |

If there are widely used alternatives, either in British or American English, these are given. Some alternatives are characteristic of British regional accents, and are marked †.

| data ˈdeɪt ə ˈdɑːt ə, †ˈdæt ə ‖ ˈdeɪt̬ ə ˈdæt̬ ə, ˈdɑːt̬ ə |

| bath v bɑːθ †bæθ |

Occasionally, pronunciations are shown which many English speakers use, but which many other English speakers consider incorrect. These are marked ⚠.

| ate past of eat et eɪt ‖ eɪt ⚠ et |

(In American English et is considered incorrect.)

The dictionary entries below are labelled to show the pronunciations given.

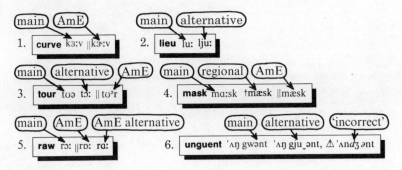

1. curve kɜːv ‖kɝːv (main) (AmE)
2. lieu luː ljuː (main) (alternative)
3. tour tʊə tɔː ‖ tʊªr (main) (alternative) (AmE)
4. mask mɑːsk †mæsk ‖mæsk (main) (regional) (AmE)
5. raw rɔː ‖rɒː rɑː (main) (AmE) (AmE alternative)
6. unguent ˈʌŋ gwənt ˈʌŋ gjuˌənt, ⚠ ˈʌndʒ ənt (main) (alternative) ('incorrect')

EXERCISE 9

AIM: TO BECOME FAMILIAR WITH THE LAYOUT OF ENTRIES, AND RECOGNISE THE TYPES OF PRONUNCIATION SHOWN.

KEY

Label the dictionary entries below, like those on page 5.

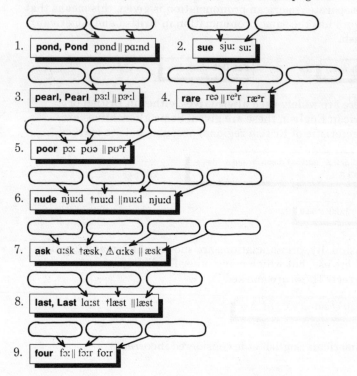

1. **pond, Pond** pɒnd ‖ pɑːnd

2. **sue** sjuː suː

3. **pearl, Pearl** pɜːl ‖ pɝːl

4. **rare** reə ‖ reᵊr ræᵊr

5. **poor** pɔː pʊə ‖ pʊᵊr

6. **nude** njuːd †nuːd ‖ nuːd njuːd

7. **ask** ɑːsk †æsk, △ɑːks ‖ æsk

8. **last, Last** lɑːst †læst ‖ læst

9. **four** fɔː ‖ fɔːr foːr

EXERCISE 10

AIM: TO RECOGNISE THE TYPES OF PRONUNCIATION GIVEN, AND PRACTISE TRANSCRIBING THEM.

KEY

Study the dictionary entries printed below.
Then use the information to complete the boxes on the following page.

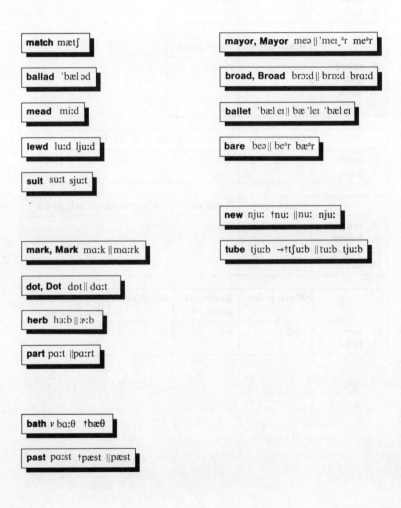

match mætʃ

ballad ˈbæl əd

mead miːd

lewd luːd ljuːd

suit suːt sjuːt

mark, Mark mɑːk ‖ mɑːrk

dot, Dot dɒt ‖ dɑːt

herb hɜːb ‖ ɜ˞ːb

part pɑːt ‖ pɑːrt

bath v bɑːθ †bæθ

past pɑːst †pæst ‖ pæst

mayor, Mayor meə ‖ ˈmeɪ ˌə˞r meə˞r

broad, Broad brɔːd ‖ brɒːd brɑːd

ballet ˈbæl eɪ ‖ bæ ˈleɪ ˈbæl eɪ

bare beə ‖ beə˞r bæə˞r

new njuː †nuː ‖ nuː njuː

tube tjuːb →tʃuːb ‖ tuːb tjuːb

KEY

	Main pron
1. match 2. ballad 3. mead	mætʃ

	Main pron	Alternative pron
4. lewd 5. suit	luːd	ljuːd

	Main pron	AmE pron
6. mark 7. dot 8. herb 9. part	mɑːk	mɑːrk

	Main pron	Regional pron	AmE pron
10. bath 11. past	bɑːθ	bæθ	bæθ

	Main pron	AmE pron	Alternative AmE pron
12. mayor 13. broad 14. ballet 15. bare	meə	meɪˌ°r	meᵊr

	Main pron	Regional pron	AmE pron	Alternative AmE pron
16. new 17. tube	njuː	nuː	nuː	njuː

EXERCISE 11

AIM: TO IDENTIFY WHICH PRONUNCIATION OF A WORD IS USED, WHEN YOU HEAR IT.

Listen to the speakers on the cassette. Notice their pronunciation of the words studied on pages 7–8. Transcribe the words as they pronounce them, and identify which of the variant pronunciations they use. You might like to say whether you think each speaker is English or American. The first one is done for you.

KEY

	Transcription	Which pron?	English or American?
Speaker 1: mark	mɑːk	main	English with a regional accent
past	pæst	regional (or AmE)	
mayor			
Speaker 2: tour			
part			
poor			
Speaker 3: rare			
new			
suit			
ballet			
Speaker 4: Tube			
last			
four			

For those interested in studying some of the differences between American and British English pronunciation, there is a section on American pronunciation on pages 65–70. Regional pronunciations are discussed in LPD Introduction 2.2.

3 Alternative pronunciations

In order to present information concisely, alternative pronunciations are often abbreviated. To get the most out of the dictionary, it is important to be able to interpret the conventions which are used.

EXERCISE 12

DIAGNOSTIC EXERCISE IN INTERPRETING INFORMATION ABOUT ALTERNATIVE PRONUNCIATIONS.

How many pronunciations are represented in this entry from the dictionary?

> **beautiful** ˈbjuːt əf ᵊl -ɪf-; -ɪ fʊl, -ə- ‖ ˈbjuːt̬-

KEY

When you have worked out what you think, check your answer in the key.

If you got the right answer, you made good use of the conventions which enable the dictionary to present so much information in such a small space. You do not need to work through exercises 13–16. Go straight on to page 15.

If you didn't spot all the pronunciations of **beautiful**, you might like to go back now and try to work them out for yourself before you look at the details below and listen to the pronunciations on the cassette.

ˈbjuːt	əf ᵊl	- ɪf-;	-ɪ fʊl, -ə- ‖	ˈ bjuː t̬-
1 2	3 4	5	6	7 – 12

1. The main pronunciation, the one recommended to foreign learners, is ˈbjuːt əf l

2. Alternative pronunciation: ˈbjuːt əf əl
   The other alternatives all have the same first syllable as the main pronunciation, so this syllable is not repeated; it is replaced by a hyphen ( ).

3. & 4. An alternative pronunciation of the middle syllable: ˈbjuːt ɪf l   ˈbjuːt ɪf əl

5. An alternative pronunciation – a different pronunciation of the final syllable: ˈbjuːt ɪ fʊl

6. The same first and last syllable as 5 with a different middle syllable: 'bju:t ə fʊl

The American pronunciation has a different allophone of t in the first syllable. The main American pronunciation is therefore:

7. 'bju:t̬ əf l

The alternative pronunciations of the middle and last syllables shown in 2–6 also occur in American pronunciations, so alternatives exist:

8. 'bju:t̬ əf əl

9. 'bju:t̬ ɪf l

10. 'bju:t̬ ɪf əl

11. 'bju:t̬ ɪ fʊl

12. 'bju:t̬ ə fʊl

The example above shows how much information a brief entry can contain. The conventions for showing alternative pronunciations are studied systematically in the rest of this section.

EXERCISES 13–17

AIM: TO UNDERSTAND THE CONVENTIONS USED TO ABBREVIATE ALTERNATIVE PRONUNCIATIONS FOLLOWING THE MAIN PRONUNCIATION.

When alternative pronunciations differ only in one syllable, the dictionary shows the part of the word which is different, and the rest of the word is 'cut back'.

Alternatives at the beginning of a word

astrology ə 'strɒl ədʒ i ⟨æ-⟩ ‖-'strɑːl-

This means that there is an alternative pronunciation, æ'strɒl ədʒ i. Only the first syllable is different. This is given in the dictionary, and the rest of the pronunciation is represented by a hyphen ( ).

EXERCISE 13

The following words all have one or more alternative
pronunciations of the first syllable. (The number in brackets
shows the number of alternatives.)
a. Can you think what the alternatives are? Write what you
   think.
b. Look the words up in the dictionary, and note the alternatives
   shown. Correct what you wrote, if necessary.

1. **accept** ək'sept (2) ....

2. **behave** bɪ'heɪv (2) ....

3. **desolation** ˌdes ə'leɪ ʃn (1) ....

4. **economic** ˌiːk ə'nɒm ɪk (1) ....

5. **exult** ɪg'zʌlt (5) ....

Alternatives at the end of a word

manag|e 'mæn ɪdʒ (-ədʒ)

This means that there is an alternative pronunciation
'mæn ədʒ. The first syllable, which is the same, is not repeated;
instead it is replaced by a hyphen.

astronaut 'æs trə nɔːt ‖ (-nɒːt -nɑːt)

This means that Americans pronounce the final syllable with a
different vowel; the final syllable is given (with an alternative),
and the first two syllables, which are the same as the main
English pronunciation, are replaced by a hyphen.

EXERCISE 14

The following words all have one or more alternative pronunciations of the last syllable. (The number in brackets shows the number of alternatives.)

a. Can you think what the alternatives are? Write what you think.
b. Look the words up in the dictionary, and note the alternatives shown. Correct what you wrote, if necessary.

1. **garage** 'gær ɑːʒ (2) ....

2. **kindred** 'kɪndr əd (1) ....

3. **hopeful** 'həʊp fᵊl (1) ....

4. **mistress** 'mɪs trəs (1) ....

5. **opiate** 'əʊp i‿ət (2) ....

Alternatives in the middle of a word

management 'mæn ɪdʒ mənt (-ədʒ-)

This means that there is an alternative pronunciation 'mæn ədʒ mənt. The first and last syllables are the same as the main pronunciation, so they are each replaced by a hyphen.

EXERCISE 15

The following words all have an alternative pronunciation of the middle syllable.

a. Can you think what the alternative is? Write what you think.
b. Look the words up in the dictionary, and note the alternative shown. Correct what you wrote, if necessary.

1. **secretive** 'siːk rət ɪv ....

2. **incisive** ɪn 'saɪs ɪv ....

3. **inherent** ɪn'hɪər ənt ....

4. **manager** 'mæn ɪdʒ ə ....

5. **make-believe** 'meɪk bɪˌliːv ....

Combinations of alternatives

In some words, more than one syllable has an alternative
pronunciation, and these are independent of one another. The
alternative syllables marked in the dictionary therefore
represent several combinations.

> **abseil** 'æb seɪ°l 'æp-, -saɪ°l

There are two possible first syllables, and two possible second
syllables. These can combine to make four pronunciations.

'æb ⎱ ⎰ seɪ°l ⎱   'æb seɪ°l
              'æp seɪ°l
'æp ⎰ ⎱ saɪ°l ⎰   'æb saɪ°l
              'æp saɪ°l

EXERCISE 16

Below are a number of dictionary entries. For each entry, one of
the alternative pronunciations shown is recorded on the cassette.
For each one:

a. Transcribe the pronunciation you hear.
b. Circle the parts of the dictionary entry which show that
   pronunciation.

The first one is done for you.

1. **decision** dɪ'sɪʒ ⁿ ⓘ ⑤, †diː, 'zɪʃ, -⑤ ...**də'zɪʒn**......

2. **opposite** 'ɒp əz ɪt -əs-, †-ət‖ɑːp- ....

3. **substantial** səb'stæn'ʃ °l †sʌb-, -'stɑːn'ʃ- ....

4. **transistor** træn 'zɪst ə trɑːn-, †trən-, -'sɪst- ....

5. **decisive** dɪ'saɪs ɪv də-, †diː-, -'saɪz- ....

6. **exasperate** ɪg 'zæsp ə reɪt eg-, əg-, ɪk-, ek-, ək,
   -'zɑːsp- ....

Alternative pronunciations involving the symbol ▪

Unstressed syllables in the middle of a multisyllabic word are often shown in relation to a stressed syllable. This ensures that you know which syllable is being referred to.

> **manageab|le** ˈmæn ɪdʒ əb |ᵊl ◯ədʒ-

This square block preceded by a stress mark stands for the stressed syllable in front of the alternative pronunciation. The alternative pronunciation of the word is thus:
ˈmæn ədʒ əb ᵊl
Notice that the square block (▪) always stands for *one* syllable, whereas the hyphen (-) replacing part of a word may stand for one or more than one syllable.

> **unceremonious** ˌʌn ˌser ɪ ˈməʊn i ˌəs ◯ə-

This square block preceded by a tertiary stress mark stands for the syllable which carries tertiary stress in the main pronunciation. The alternative pronunciation is thus clearly shown as referring to the syllable following the tertiary stress. The alternative pronunciation of the word is thus:
ˌʌn ˌser ə ˈməʊn i ˌəs

> **acupuncturist** ˈæk ju ˌpʌŋk tʃər ɪst (ˈ▪ jə-)
> ▪▪ˈ▪-, -ʃər ɪst, †-əst

This alternative is shown as being in the syllable after the initial stressed syllable. Thus:
ˈæk jəˌpʌŋk tʃər ɪst

EXERCISE 17

KEY Use the dictionary to help you say and transcribe the following:

1. The American pronunciation of **Aberdeen**, in Scotland.
2. All the alternative pronunciations shown for **academician**.
3. The pronunciation of **Addis Ababa**.
4. The second pronunciation of **manageress**.
5. A regional pronunciation of **misrepresentation**.

EXERCISE 18
QUIZ ON ALTERNATIVE PRONUNCIATIONS.

KEY Use the dictionary to answer the following questions.

1. Can **exorcise** be pronounced like **exercise**?
2. How many British and American pronunciations exist for **majority**? Transcribe each one.
3. **mandatory** – is the pronunciation mæn 'deɪt ər i used in America?
4. TRUE OR FALSE?   'Nobody uses /s/ in the middle of **appreciate**.'
5. TRUE OR FALSE?   '**acotelydon** is sometimes pronounced with three ə's.'

4 Inflected and derived words

The dictionary shows how inflected and derived words are pronounced. One-syllable words are shown in full. For others, both the spelling and pronunciation are shown as endings following a headword.

```
reason, R~  'ri:z ²n  ~ed d  ~ing/s ˌɪŋ/z
   ~s z
reasonab|le  'ri:z ²n ˌəb |²l  ~ly li  ~ness nəs
   nɪs
reassess ˌri:ˌə 'ses  ~ed t  ~es ɪz əz
   ~ing ɪŋ  ~ment/s mənt/s
reassign ˌri:ˌə 'saɪn  ~ed d  ~ing ɪŋ  ~s z
reas|sure ˌri:ˌə |'ʃɔ: -'ʃʊə; rɪə'· ‖-|'ʃʊ²r -'ʃɜ:
   ~sured 'ʃɔ:d 'ʃʊəd ‖'ʃʊ²rd 'ʃɜ:d
   ~sures 'ʃɔ:z 'ʃʊəz ‖'ʃʊ²rz 'ʃɜ:z
   ~suring/ly 'ʃɔ:r ɪŋ /li 'ʃʊər- ‖'ʃʊr ɪŋ /li
   'ʃɜ:-
reassuranc|e ˌri:ˌə 'ʃʊər ən's -'ʃɔ:r- ‖-'ʃʊr-
   -'ʃɜ:-  ~es ɪz əz
Reaumur, Réaumur 'reɪ əʊ mjʊə
   ‖ˌreɪ oʊ 'mjʊ²r  —Fr [ʁe o my:ʁ]
Reave ri:v
reawaken ˌri:ˌə 'weɪk ən  ~ed d  ~ing ˌɪŋ
   ~s z
```

```
reason, R~  'ri:z ²n  ~ed d  ~ing/s ˌɪŋ/z
   ~s z
```

In the spelling of this example, endings are added to the headword with no alteration. For the pronunciation of inflected words, just add the pronunciation of the endings.

Thus: **reasoned** ri:z ²nd
  reasoning 'ri:z ²nˌɪŋ
  reasonings 'ri:z ²nˌɪŋz
  reasons 'ri:z ²nz

Sometimes an ending is added not to the complete word but to just part of it. The symbol | is used to show exactly which part is concerned.

> **reasonab|le** ˈriːz ᵊn‿əb |ᵊl ~**ly** li ~**ness** nəs
> nɪs

reasonab + ly   ˈriːz ᵊn‿əb + li
= reasonably   = ˈriːz ᵊn‿əb li

> **reassuranc|e** ˌriː‿ə ˈʃʊər ən's -ˈʃɔːr- ‖-ˈʃʊr-
> -ˈʃɜː- ~**es** ɪz əz

reassuranc + es   ˌriː‿ə ˈʃʊər ən's + ɪz
= reassurances   ˌriː‿ə ˈʃʊər ən's ɪz

EXERCISE 19

AIM: TO UNDERSTAND THE CONVENTIONS USED IN THE DICTIONARY TO SHOW THE SPELLING AND PRONUNCIATION OF INFLECTED AND DERIVED WORDS.
TO TRANSCRIBE THE PRONUNCIATIONS.

KEY

Find the following words in the dictionary extract on page 17, and transcribe their pronunciation.

1. **reassessment** ....
2. **reassigned** ....
3. **reassuring** ....
4. **reawakens** ....

EXERCISE 20

QUIZ ON INFLECTED AND DERIVED FORMS.

KEY

Use the dictionary to help you answer the following questions.

1. What is the American pronunciation of **marketed**?
2. How is **kindliness** pronounced – ˈkaɪnd li nəs or ˈkaɪnd lə nəs?
3. Which is the correct pronunciation of **uselessly** –
   ˈjuːs ləs li or juːz ləs li?
4. TRUE OR FALSE? 'The words **studied** and **studded** are sometimes pronounced the same.'
5. How is the plural of **agency** pronounced –
   ˈeɪdʒ əns iz or ˈeɪdʒ əns əz?

EXERCISES 21–22

AIM: TO APPLY YOUR UNDERSTANDING OF LAYOUT OF ENTRIES, ALTERNATIVE PRONUNCIATIONS, INFLECTIONS AND DERIVED FORMS.

EXERCISE 21

KEY

Look up in the dictionary the words listed below, and complete the table. The first two are done for you.

	Main	Alternative	Regional	AmE	AmE alternative
1. Asia	ˈeɪʃə	ˈeɪʒə		ˈeɪʒə	ˈeɪʃə
2. nothing	ˈnʌθɪŋ		ˈnɒθɪŋ		
3. Aberdaron					
4. ballroom					
5. behave					
6. economics					
7. managing					
8. target					

EXERCISE 22

KEY

Look up in the dictionary the words listed below, and complete the table. The first two are done for you.

	Main	Alternative	Regional	'Incorrect'	AmE	AmE alternative
1. topmast	ˈtɒp mɑːst	ˈtɒp məst	ˈtɒp mæst		ˈtɑːp mæst	
2. arthritis	ɑː ˈθraɪt ɪs		ɑː ˈθraɪt əs	ɑːθ əˈraɪt ɪs	ɑːr ˈθraɪt əs	
3. Buckingham						
4. dancing						
5. mistake						
6. Saturday						
7. tariff						
8. trauma						

5 Optional sounds

1 **Optional sounds** are sounds which are pronounced by some speakers or on some occasions, but are omitted by other speakers or on other occasions. In LPD they are indicated in two ways: by **italics** and by **raised** letters.

2 Sounds shown in **italics** are sounds which the foreign learner is recommended to include (although native speakers sometimes omit them). They denote sounds which may optionally be **elided** (omitted).
lunch ˈlʌnʧ   Some say lʌnʧ, others say lʌnʃ. LPD recommends lʌnʧ.
bacon ˈbeɪk ən   Some say ˈbeɪk ən, others say ˈbeɪk n. LPD recommends ˈbeɪk ən.

3 Sounds shown with **raised letters** are sounds which the foreign learner is recommended to ignore (although native speakers sometimes include them). They denote sounds which may optionally be **inserted**.
fence fenˢs   Some say fens, others say fents. LPD recommends fens.
sadden ˈsæd ᵊn Some say ˈsæd n, others say ˈsæd ən. LPD recommends ˈsæd n.

Sounds shown in italics: elision

Elision is the omission (= deletion) of a sound that would otherwise be present. It is particularly characteristic of rapid or casual speech.

EXERCISE 23
AIM: TO IDENTIFY THE FULL AND ELIDED PRONUNCIATION OF WORDS WHEN YOU HEAR THEM.

a. The words below all have a sound which can be elided (omitted, deleted). Listen to the cassette: each word is spoken twice, first in full, and then with elision.

	in full	with elision
1. French	frenʧ	frenʃ
2. plunge	plʌnʤ	plʌnʒ
3. stamped	stæmpt	stæmt
4. tangerine	ˌtænʤ ə ˈriːn	ˌtænʒ ə ˈriːn
5. tasteful	ˈteɪst fʊl	ˈteɪs fʊl
6. kindness	ˈkaɪnd nəs	ˈkaɪn nəs
7. awaken	ə ˈweɪk ən	ə ˈweɪk n

b. Listen to the words on the cassette. For each word circle the appropriate transcription in a. above.

21

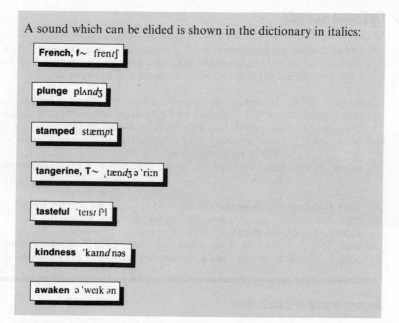

A sound which can be elided is shown in the dictionary in italics:

French, f~ fren*t*ʃ

plunge plʌn*d*ʒ

stamped stæm*p*t

tangerine, T~ ˌtæn*d*ʒ ə ˈriːn

tasteful ˈteɪs*t* f*ə*l

kindness ˈkaɪn*d* nəs

awaken ə ˈweɪk *ə*n

EXERCISE 24
AIM: TO UNDERSTAND THE MARKING OF ELISION IN THE DICTIONARY.

The dictionary entries below show that elision may take place in these words. Look at the transcriptions next to the entries. For each one, mark whether the word is given in full (F) or with elision (E). The first one is done for you.

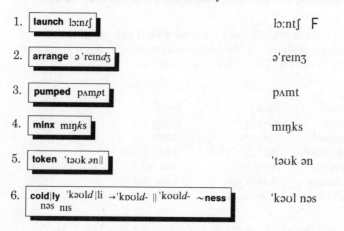

1. **launch** lɔːn*t*ʃ   lɔːntʃ F

2. **arrange** ə ˈreɪn*d*ʒ   əˈreɪnʒ

3. **pumped** pʌm*p*t   pʌmt

4. **minx** mɪŋ*k*s   mɪŋks

5. **token** ˈtəʊk ən‖   ˈtəʊk ən

6. **cold|ly** ˈkəʊl*d* |li →ˈkʊʊld- ‖ ˈkəʊld- **~ness**   ˈkəʊl nəs
   nəs nɪs

EXERCISES 25–26

AIM: TO UNDERSTAND THE CONDITIONS IN WHICH ELISION OF CONSONANTS TAKES PLACE,
AND SO TO PREDICT WHEN ELISION MAY TAKE PLACE.
TO SAY AND TRANSCRIBE FULL AND ELIDED FORMS.

Elision of consonants

Within a syllable:
t may be elided in ntʃ   e.g. **lunch** lʌntʃ, lʌnʃ
d may be elided in ndʒ   e.g. **strange** streɪndʒ, streɪnʒ
p may be elided in mps, mpt   e.g. **jumped** dʒʌmpt, dʒʌmt
t may be elided in nts   e.g. **contents** 'kɒn tents, 'kɒn tens
k may be elided in ŋks, ŋkt   e.g. **lynx** lɪŋks, lɪŋs
At the end of a syllable, t and d may be elided before a
consonant in the next syllable:
t may be elided in ft, st   e.g. **firstly** 'fɜːst li, 'fɜːs li
and less commonly in pt, kt, tʃt, θt, ʃt
d may be elided in ld, nd   e.g. **baldness** 'bɔːld nəs, 'bɔːl nəs
and less commonly in bd, gd, dʒd, vd, ðd, zd, md, ŋd

EXERCISE 25

KEY 📼

Say and transcribe the following words in their full form, and
with elision. You can check the pronunciation on the cassette,
and the transcription in the key.

in full   *with elision*

1. **pinch**
2. **bandstand**
3. **camped**
4. **wistful**
5. **softness**
6. **textbook**

EXERCISE 26

KEY

Four of the following words can exhibit elision. Circle those
words.

softly   softer   customer   lounge   firstly   judged lateness   wasteful

There is further discussion of elision in the note ELISION in
LPD.

Sounds shown by raised letters: insertion

Insertion of consonants

Some words have an alternative pronunciation in which a consonant is inserted. The inserted sound is shown by a small, raised letter.

	Main pron	*with insertion*
prince, P~ prɪnˈs	prɪns	prɪnts (= prints)
triumph *n, v,* **T~** ˈtraɪ ʌmᵖf	ˈtraɪ ʌmf	ˈtraɪ ʌmpf

These consonants are only inserted after a nasal sound, when the vocal organs are not precisely synchronised in their movement from the position for the nasal to the position for the following oral sound.

EXERCISE 27

AIM: TO IDENTIFY WHETHER A SOUND HAS BEEN INSERTED, WHEN YOU HEAR A WORD.

The dictionary entries below show that the words are sometimes pronounced with an inserted sound. Listen to the words on the cassette, and transcribe the pronunciations you hear.

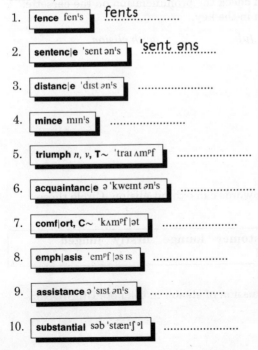

1. **fence** fenˈs   *fents*

2. **sentenc|e** ˈsent ənˈs   *ˈsent əns*

3. **distanc|e** ˈdɪst ənˈs   ....

4. **mince** mɪnˈs   ....

5. **triumph** *n, v,* **T~** ˈtraɪ ʌmᵖf   ....

6. **acquaintanc|e** əˈkweɪnt ənˈs   ....

7. **comf|ort, C~** ˈkʌmᵖf |ət   ....

8. **emph|asis** ˈemᵖf |əs ɪs   ....

9. **assistance** əˈsɪst ənˈs   ....

10. **substantial** səbˈstænˈʃ əl   ....

Insertion of ə

This is an alternative to a syllabic consonant, and is dealt with in the section on syllabic consonants on pages 26–30.

EXERCISE 28

AIM: TO APPLY KNOWLEDGE OF OPTIONAL SOUNDS IN STUDYING A CONVERSATION.

The conversation below is recorded on the cassette. You can use it as you choose. Three different approaches are suggested.

Suggestion 1. Before you listen, read the conversation and underline the words in which elision or insertion are possible. Use Key A to check what you have marked.

KEY

Then listen to the conversation on the cassette to see how the speakers pronounce these words; circle those which have undergone elision or insertion. Use Key B to check.

KEY

Suggestion 2. Listen to the conversation, with the book closed, and transcribe it. You can use Key B to check your transcription.

KEY

Suggestion 3. When you have listened to the conversation, (and followed suggestion 1 or 2), practise saying the conversation. Record yourself, and compare your version with the one on the cassette.

A: I've just had my lounge decorated. It hadn't been done since I moved in.
B: What colour is it?
A: It's called French Blush.
B: Very tasteful, I'm sure, but it doesn't convey anything.
A: Well, on the chart it looked lovely – a sort of pale tangerine colour.
B: That sounds nice. The lounge faces north, doesn't it, and a tangerine glow would take away the coldness.
A: That's just what I thought: elegant but comfortable. But actually it's more like orange. It's cheerful – but not very restful.

6 Syllabic consonants

1 Most syllables contain a vowel sound. Sometimes, though, a syllable consists only of a consonant (or consonants). If so, this consonant (or one of them) is a nasal (usually n) or liquid (l or, especially in AmE, r). For example, in the usual pronunciation of **suddenly** ˈsʌd n li, the second syllable consists of n alone. Such a consonant is called a **syllabic consonant**.

2 Instead of a syllabic consonant it is always possible to pronounce a vowel ə plus an ordinary (non-syllabic) consonant. Thus it is possible, though not usual, to say ˈsʌd ən li rather than ˈsʌd n li.

EXERCISE 29
AIM: TO RECOGNISE SYLLABLES CONTAINING A SYLLABIC CONSONANT OR VOWEL + CONSONANT, WHEN YOU HEAR AND SEE THEM.

a. The words below all have a main pronunciation with a syllabic consonant. Listen to the cassette: each word is spoken twice, first with a syllabic consonant, and then with a vowel + consonant.

		syllabic consonant	*vowel + consonant*
1.	**suddenly**	ˈsʌd n li	ˈsʌd ən li
2.	**Britain**	ˈbrɪt n	ˈbrɪt ən
3.	**frightening**	ˈfraɪt n ɪŋ	ˈfraɪt ən ɪŋ
4.	**hidden**	ˈhɪd n	ˈhɪd ən
5.	**medal**	ˈmed l	ˈmed əl
6.	**needlework**	ˈniːd l wɜːk	ˈniːd əl wɜːk
7.	**cattle**	ˈkæt l	ˈkæt əl
8.	**petals**	ˈpet·lz	ˈpet əlz
9.	**panel**	ˈpæn l	ˈpæn əl
10.	**softener**	ˈsɒf n ə	ˈsɒf ən ə
11.	**station**	ˈsteɪ ʃn	ˈsteɪ ʃən
12.	**fastened**	ˈfɑːs nd	ˈfɑːs ənd

b. Listen to the words on the cassette. For each word, circle the appropriate transcription in a. above.

KEY

EXERCISE 30

AIM: TO RECOGNISE CONTEXTS IN WHICH SYLLABIC CONSONANTS ARE LIKELY.
TO IDENTIFY AND TRANSCRIBE SYLLABLES CONTAINING A SYLLABIC CONSONANT OR
VOWEL + CONSONANT, WHEN YOU HEAR WORDS.

KEY a. Look at the text below. Underline words which are likely to
        contain syllabic consonants. Use Key A to check the words
        you have underlined.

KEY b. Listen to the text on the cassette and notice how the speaker
        pronounces each word you have underlined: does it have a
        syllabic consonant? Transcribe these words as spoken on the
        · cassette. Use Key B to check.

GOLDEN OLDIES-
the most popular songs chosen by radio listeners:

The Battle of New Orleans
Wooden Heart
Beautiful Dreamer
I Beg your Pardon (I never promised you a rose garden)
The Tunnel of Love
Sentimental Journey
Suddenly it's Spring
Congratulations

3   Likely syllabic consonants are shown in LPD with the symbol ᵊ, thus **suddenly** 'sʌd ᵊn li. LPD's regular principle is that a raised symbol indicates a sound whose insertion LPD does not recommend (see OPTIONAL SOUNDS). Hence this notation implies that LPD prefers bare n in the second syllable. Since there is then no proper vowel in this syllable, the n must be syllabic.

4   Similarly, in **middle** 'mɪd ᵊl LPD recommends a pronunciation with syllabic l, thus 'mɪd l. In **father** 'fɑːð ə‖ 'fɑːð ᵊr LPD recommends for AmE a pronunciation with syllabic r, thus 'fɑːð r.

5   The IPA provides a special diacritic ˌ to show a syllabic consonant, thus n̩, 'sʌdn̩li. For AmE syllabic r, the symbol ɚ is sometimes used, thus 'fɑːðɚ. Because LPD uses spaces to show syllabification, it does not need these conventions. Any nasal or liquid in a syllable in which there is no other vowel must automatically be syllabic.

Since it is always possible to insert ə in a word with a syllabic consonant, words containing syllabic consonants in the dictionary are all shown with ᵊ, as shown in the following entries.

sudden 'sʌd ᵊn ~ly li

Britain 'brɪt ᵊn

frighten 'fraɪt ᵊn
~ing/ly ɪŋ /li

hidden 'hɪd ᵊn

medal 'med ᵊl

needlework 'niːd ᵊl wɜːk

cattle 'kæt ᵊl ‖'kæt̬ ᵊl

petal 'pet ᵊl ‖ 'peṭ ᵊl ~ed, ~led ᵈ ~s ᶻ

panel 'pæn ᵊl

softener 'sɒf ᵊn ̯ə

station 'steɪʃ ᵊn

fasten 'fɑːs ᵊn †'fæs- ‖ 'fæs ᵊn ~ed ᵈ

What is the difference between ən and ᵊn?

Remember the conventions used in the dictionary:
– an italic letter shows a sound which is sometimes elided. The main pronunciation – which foreign learners are recommended to use – *includes* the sound. So for

distant 'dɪst ənt

the recommended pronunciation is dɪst ənt

– a raised letter shows a sound which is sometimes inserted. The main pronunciation *does not include* this sound. So for

button, B~ 'bʌt ᵊn

the recommended pronunciation is bʌt n

EXERCISE 31

AIM: TO INTERPRET THE SYMBOLS ᵊ AND ə QUICKLY AND CORRECTLY.

In some of the following words, the recommended pronunciation has a syllabic consonant. In others, the recommended pronunciation has a syllable with ə. Look up each word in the dictionary; then transcribe its recommended pronunciation. The first one is done for you.

KEY

1. absent   'æb sn̩t........
2. beckon   ....
3. current   ....
4. cycle   ....
5. Pamela   ....
6. paragon   ....
7. servant   ....
8. similar   ....
9. traveller   ....
10. vacant   ....

7 Compression

1 Sometimes a sequence of sounds in English has two possible pronunciations: either as two separate syllables, or **compressed** into a single syllable. Possible compressions are shown in LPD by the symbol ⁀ between the syllables affected.

E.g. **lenient** 'liːn i‿ənt   Two pronunciations are possible: a slower one 'liːn i ənt, and a faster one 'liːn jənt.

diagram 'daɪ‿ə græm   Two pronunciations are possible: a slower one 'daɪ ə græm, and a faster one 'daə græm. *

maddening 'mæd ᵊn‿ɪŋ   Two pronunciations are possible: a slower one with three syllables, 'mæd n ɪŋ or 'mæd ən ɪŋ, and a faster one with two syllables, 'mæd nɪŋ

2 Generally the uncompressed version is more usual

● in rarer words
● in slow or deliberate speech
● the first time the word occurs in a discourse.

The compressed pronunciation is more usual
● in frequently-used words
● in fast or casual speech
● if the word has already been used in the discourse.

Compression involving a consonant

Compression causes a possible syllabic consonant to become a plain non-syllabic consonant.
A frequent context for compression is when -ing is added to a verb ending with a syllabic consonant. The inflected form often appears in the dictionary under the verb, with the ending shown separately.

battl|e, B~ ('bæt ᵊl) ||'bæt̬ ᵊl   **~ed** d   **~es** z
   ~ing (ɪŋ)

This represents an entry
battling bæt ᵊl‿ɪŋ
which can be pronounced with three syllables or two syllables.

EXERCISE 32

AIM: TO CHECK YOUR UNDERSTANDING OF THE CONVENTIONS SHOWN ABOVE.

Say and transcribe the pronunciations of **battling** with three syllables and two syllables. You can check the pronunciations on the cassette, and the transcriptions in the key.

EXERCISE 33

AIM: TO RECOGNISE WHETHER A WORD HAS UNDERGONE COMPRESSION WHEN YOU HEAR THE WORD.

Listen to the words below, on the cassette. For each one, decide if it is pronounced with three syllables, i.e. has a syllabic consonant in the middle, or if it is pronounced with two syllables, i.e. has undergone compression. Write how many syllables you hear. The first two are done for you.

1. **maddening** .3..
2. **battling** 2..
3. **flattening** ....
4. **sprinkling** ....
5. **cycling** ....
6. **reckoning** ....
7. **threatening** ....
8. **trickling** ....

EXERCISE 34

AIM: TO TRANSCRIBE WORDS CONTAINING A SYLLABIC CONSONANT PLUS SUFFIX, SHOWING WHETHER THE SYLLABIC CONSONANT HAS UNDERGONE COMPRESSION.

Transcribe the words on the cassette in exercise 33, making sure you show whether there is a syllabic consonant or whether it has undergone compression.

EXERCISE 35

AIM: TO USE THE DICTIONARY TO CHECK WHETHER COMPRESSION CAN TAKE PLACE.

The following words all have a main pronunciation with three syllables. In some of the words, compression sometimes takes place and they are pronounced with two syllables.

---

finally   traveller   carefully   globally   lengthening
normally   nursery   sampling   summarise   totally
tunnelling

Look up each word in the dictionary and check whether it is marked for compression. Complete the table on the next page. The first two are done for you.

KEY		
	Words with no compression: always three syllables e.g. **finally** 'faɪn ᵊl i	Words with compression: can be two syllables e.g. **traveller** 'træv ᵊl‿ə
	faɪn ᵊl i	'træv lə

Compression involving a vowel

Where compression is marked between vowels, the two vowels can be compressed into one syllable. The details of the phonetic changes possible are given in the LPD note: COMPRESSION, para. 7.

EXERCISE 36

AIM: TO RECOGNISE FULL AND COMPRESSED FORMS WHEN YOU HEAR AND SEE THEM.

a. The words below can all undergo compression. Listen to the cassette: each word is spoken twice, first in full and then with two syllables compressed into one.

		full	*with compression*
1.	**obvious** 'ɒb vi‿əs	'ɒb vi əs	'ɒb vjəs
2.	**bicentennial** ˌbaɪ sen 'ten i‿əl	ˌbaɪ sən 'ten i əl	ˌbaɪ sen 'ten jəl
3.	**studious** 'stjuːd i‿əs	'stjuːd i əs	'stjuːd jəs
4.	**usual** 'juːʒ u‿əl	'juːʒ u əl	'juːʒ wəl

5. 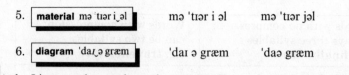 material mə 'tɪər i əl   mə 'tɪər i əl   mə 'tɪər jəl

6. diagram 'daɪ̯ə græm   'daɪ ə græm   'daə græm

b. Listen to the words on the cassette. For each word, circle the appropriate transcription in a. above.

EXERCISE 37

AIM: TO IDENTIFY WHETHER WORDS HAVE UNDERGONE COMPRESSION WHEN YOU HEAR THEM.

The words below can all undergo compression. Listen to them on the cassette, and write F for full, or C for compressed. The first two are done for you.

1. **cafeteria** F
2. **diabetes** C
3. **previous**
4. **proprietor**
5. **fastidious**
6. **affluent**
7. **residual**
8. **obedient**
9. **curious**

EXERCISE 38

AIM: TO RECOGNISE SYLLABIC CONSONANTS AND COMPRESSION IN A CONVERSATION.

Listen to the conversation on the cassette. Can you find the following?

Eight words with syllabic consonants.
Two words with compression involving a consonant.
Five words with compression involving vowels.

A: These plants haven't flowered at all this year. I bought them from a reputable company, but I think they must be rotten.

B: This label says they are biennials.

A: So they ought to flower twice a year.

B: No, those are biannuals. Biennial plants only flower every other year. Your plants obviously aren't flowering because this is the first year.

A: I thought a biennial was a sort of two-hundred year anniversary. 1989 was the biennial of the French Revolution, and there was a great celebration in Paris.

B: No, you are thinking of bicentennial.

A: Oh, the advantages of a classical education!

B STRESS IN WORDS AND PHRASES

This part of the book deals with the marking of stress in words and phrases. It begins with an introductory case study, focussing on one very specific use of stress patterns in words, before going on to look at the full range of stress patterns and marking. Stress is discussed in LPD in the Introduction 3.3, and the note STRESS.

8 Pairs of words with different stress

A number of English words have the same spelling for a noun or adjective and a verb. There is a group of these two-syllable words where the noun/adjective is stressed on the first syllable, and the verb on the second.

    e.g. a **record** 're kɔːd   to **record** rɪ 'kɔːd
           perfect 'pɜːf ɪkt   to **perfect** pɜː 'fekt

EXERCISE 39
AIM: TO STRESS NOUNS AND VERBS CORRECTLY.

KEY

Fill the gaps in the sentences below. The words you need are listed under the sentences. Mark the stressed syllable of each word.

1. There has been a big ˈ.ịṇcṛẹạṣẹ..... in the number of students applying to this college.
2. As a Red-Cross volunteer, she sometimes has to .... disabled people travelling across London.
3. A recent .... showed that 98% of households have colour television.
4. The council are going to .... the High Street into a pedestrian shopping centre.
5. The winning song in the Eurovision Song .... is usually pretty dull.
6. A gesture which is friendly in one country may be a deadly .... in another country.

contest	convert	escort	increase	insult	survey

EXERCISE 40

AIM: A. TO USE THE DICTIONARY TO CHECK STRESS PATTERNS.
B. TO STRESS NOUNS AND VERBS CORRECTLY.

a. The words below can all be a noun and a verb. For some of them the noun and verb have different stress (like 'record'). For others, the noun and verb have the same stress.

Underline the words which you think have different stress for the noun and verb. Use the dictionary to check your choice.

KEY

> **answer   contrast   offer   present   reject   reply**
> **transport**

b. Use each underlined word in two sentences, once as a noun and once as a verb. Make sure you say the words with the correct stress.

Vowels in unstressed syllables

In some Noun-Verb pairs, the vowel in the first syllable is different in the noun and the verb.   e.g. 're kɔːd   rɪ 'kɔːd
In other pairs, the vowel is the same.   e.g. 'ɪn sʌlt   ɪn 'sʌlt

EXERCISE 41

AIM: TO USE THE DICTIONARY TO CHECK PRONUNCIATION.

Use the dictionary to check the vowel in the first syllable of the words underlined below. Write the word and mark the stressed syllable.

1a. There has been a <u>decrease</u> in the birth rate. 'diː kriːs ......
1b. The number of members is expected to <u>decrease</u>.
    ....
2a. His business interests <u>conflict</u> with his public duty.
    ....
2b. The border dispute may lead to armed <u>conflict</u> between the two countries. ....
3a. The President had an armed <u>escort</u>. ....
3b. The receptionist will <u>escort</u> visitors to the meeting room. ....
4a. Taxes are not expected to <u>increase</u>. ....
4b. The average <u>increase</u> in earnings last year was 6%.
    ....
5a. I cannot <u>permit</u> such behaviour. ....
5b. Have you got a <u>permit</u> for that gun? ....

6a. I'm going to <u>protest</u>. ....
6b. There will be a storm of <u>protest</u>. ....
7a. The <u>rebels</u> in the hills will never surrender. ....
7b. Every child <u>rebels</u> against authority at some stage.

....

EXERCISE 42

AIM: **FURTHER PRACTICE WITH STRESS AND PRONUNCIATION IN PAIRS OF WORDS.**

Can you solve the following clues? In each pair of clues, the
words referred to have the same spelling, but different stress.
Write the spelling, and the pronunciation corresponding to each
meaning. The first one is done for you.

1. give sympathy and comfort } <u>console</u> } kən 'səʊl
   a keyboard, panel of switches } } 'kɒn səʊl

2. decline to do something } .... }
   rubbish

3. get smaller } .... }
   a formal legal agreement

4. happy, satisfied } .... }
   what is contained in something

5. pull out }
   a short passage from a } .... }
   longer text

6. disagree, protest } .... }
   a thing

7. very small } .... }
   sixty seconds

8. go away from, leave } .... }
   a place where nothing grows

KEY If you are stuck, choose from the words in Key A. The full
answers are given in Key B.

Stress on the first syllable of nouns

This is a productive pattern, and frequently appears in new
words, particularly those formed from phrasal verbs,
e.g. 'ɪn pʊt 'teɪk ɒf

39

EXERCISE 43

AIM: TO PRACTISE STRESS ON THE FIRST SYLLABLE OF NOUNS.

Can you identify the nouns defined below? They are all related to phrasal verbs. When you say the nouns, make sure the first syllable is stressed.

KEY

1. an armed bank raid _a hold-up_

2. a burglary ....

3. an appearance by a star who had retired ....

4. a sudden strike ....

5. a cinematic device where the film switches to an earlier period ....

6. a sudden period of heavy rain ....

7. a mechanical (and, metaphorically, other) failure ....

8. a ten second period immediately before the departure of a rocket ....

9. the moment of departure of a rocket ....

10. (initial) expenditure on a particular project ....

If you are stuck, choose from the nouns listed below.

**breakdown break-in comeback countdown
downpour flashback hold-up lift-off outlay
walkout**

9 Stress marking

The stresses marked in the dictionary are lexical
(= underlying = potential) stresses; the marking shows how the
word is stressed when it is spoken in isolation, and which
syllables can be accented in connected speech

EXERCISE 44

AIM: TO RECOGNISE THE STRESSED SYLLABLE WHEN YOU HEAR A WORD. TO USE THE
PRIMARY STRESS MARK ' CORRECTLY IN A WORD WITH ONE STRESSED SYLLABLE.

The extract below comes from *Down and Out in Paris and
London* by George Orwell. Orwell is describing his experience as
a tramp in London in the 1930's. Listen to the extract on the
cassette. Mark the stressed syllable in the words underlined. The
first two are done for you.

I stayed in the streets till late at night, 'keeping on the move all

the time. Dressed as I was, I was half afraid that the police

might arrest me as a vagabond, and I dared not speak to anyone,

imagining that they must notice a disparity between my accent

and my clothes. (Later I discovered that this never happened.)

My new clothes had put me instantly into a new world.

Everyone's demeanour seemed to have changed abruptly. I

helped a hawker pick up a barrow that he had upset. 'Thanks,

mate,' he said with a grin. No one had called me mate before in

my life – it was the clothes that had done it. For the first time I

noticed, too, how the attitude of women varies with a man's

clothes. When a badly dressed man passes them they shudder

away from him with a quite frank movement of disgust, as

though he were a dead cat. Clothes are powerful things. Dressed

in a tramp's clothes it is very difficult, at any rate for the first

day, not to feel that you are genuinely degraded. You might feel

the same shame, irrational but very real, your first night in

prison.

EXERCISE 45

AIM: TO USE THE PRIMARY STRESS MARK ' CORRECTLY IN A WORD WITH ONE STRESSED SYLLABLE.

Each of these definitions refers to a word in the dictionary extract below and on the next page. Find the appropriate word, and write its transcription, with the stress marked. The first one is done for you.

KEY

1. a business that makes its money esp. by bringing people into touch with others or the products of others 'eɪdʒ əns i
2. a list of subjects to be dealt with or talked about at a meeting ....
3. to make (a difficult situation) more serious or dangerous; make worse ....
4. a person whose job is to represent another person, a company, etc. esp. one who brings people into touch with others or deals with the business affairs of a person or company ....
5. *derog* always ready to quarrel or attack ....
6. *BrE sl* trouble, esp. fighting, eg between groups of young people ....
7. an .... language: one in which words are formed by agglutination
8. able to move quickly and easily ....
9. *noun usu. derog* increase in size, power or rank, esp. when intentionally planned ....

---

agenc|y 'eɪdʒ ən's |i ~**ies** iz
agenda ə'dʒend ə ~**s** z
agene 'eɪdʒ iːn
agent 'eɪdʒ ənt ~**s** s —*see also phrases with this word*
agent provocateur ˌæʒ ɒ̃ prə ˌvɒk ə 'tɜː
ˌeɪdʒ ənt- ‖ ˌɑːʒ ɑ̃ː proʊ ˌvɑːk ə 'tɜː -'tʊ³r
— *Fr* [a ʒɑ̃ pʀɔ vɔ ka tœːʀ] **agents provocateurs** *same pronunciation, or* -z
agentive 'eɪdʒ ənt ɪv
age-old ˌeɪdʒ 'əʊld ◄ →-'ɒʊld ‖ -'oʊld ◄
-ageous 'eɪdʒ əs —*This suffix may impose rhythmic stress on the preceding stem* (ˌadvan'tageous).
ageratum ˌædʒ ə 'reɪt əm -'reɪ̯- ~**s** z
Agfa *tdmk* -'æg fə
Agg æg
Aggett 'æg ɪt -ət
Aggie 'æg i
aggiornamento ə ˌdʒɔːn ə 'ment əʊ ˌæ-
‖ ə ˌdʒɔːrn ə 'ment oʊ —*It*
[ad dʒoɾ na 'men to]

agglome|rate *v* ə ˈglɒm ə |reɪt ǁ ə ˈglɑːm-
  ~**rated** reɪt ɪd -əd ǁ reɪt̬ əd ~**rates** reɪts
  ~**rating** reɪt ɪŋ ǁ reɪt̬ ɪŋ
agglomerate *adj, n* ə ˈglɒm ər ət -ɪt, -ə reɪt
  ǁ ə ˈglɑːm- ~**s** s
agglomeration ə ˌglɒm ə ˈreɪʃ ən ǁ ə ˌglɑːm-
  ~**s** z
aggluti|nate *v* ə ˈgluːt ɪ |neɪt -ə- ǁ -ən eɪt
  ~**nated** neɪt ɪd -əd ǁ neɪt̬ əd ~**nates**
  neɪts ~**nating** neɪt ɪŋ ǁ neɪt̬ ɪŋ
agglutinate *adj, n* ə ˈgluːt ɪn ət -ən-, -ɪt;
  -ɪ neɪt, -ə- ǁ -ən- ~**s** s
agglutination ə ˌgluːt ɪ ˈneɪʃ ən -ə- ǁ -ən ˈeɪʃ-
agglutinative ə ˈgluːt ɪn ət ɪv · ˈ·ən-; -ɪ neɪt-,
  -ə neɪt-, -ən eɪt- ǁ -ən eɪt̬ ɪv -ən ət̬ ɪv ~**ly** li
aggrandis... —*see* **aggrandiz...**
aggrandiz|e ə ˈgrænd aɪz ˈæg rən daɪz ~**ed**
  d ~**es** ɪz əz ~**ing** ɪŋ
aggrandizement ə ˈgrænd ɪz mənt -əz-, -aɪz-
aggra|vate ˈæg rə |veɪt ~**vated** veɪt ɪd -əd
  ǁ veɪt̬ əd ~**vates** veɪts ~**vating/ly**
  veɪt ɪŋ /li ǁ veɪt̬ ɪŋ /li
aggravation ˌæg rə ˈveɪʃ ən ~**s** z
aggregate *adj, n* ˈæg rɪg ət -rəg-, -ɪt; -rɪ geɪt,
  -rə- ~**s** s
aggre|gate *v* ˈæg rɪ |geɪt -rə- ~**gated**
  geɪt ɪd -əd ǁ geɪt̬ əd ~**gates** geɪts
  ~**gating** geɪt ɪŋ ǁ geɪt̬ ɪŋ
aggregation ˌæg rɪ ˈgeɪʃ ən -rə- ~**s** z
aggression ə ˈgreʃ ən
aggressive ə ˈgres ɪv ~**ly** li ~**ness** nəs nɪs
aggressor ə ˈgres ə ǁ -ər ~**s** z
aggrieved ə ˈgriːvd
aggro ˈæg rəʊ ǁ -roʊ
Agha- *comb. form in Irish place names* ˈæx ə
  —**Aghacully** ˌæx ə ˈkʌl i
aghast ə ˈgɑːst †-ˈgæst ǁ ə ˈgæst
agile ˈædʒ aɪəl ǁ -əl -aɪəl *(not* ·ˈ·*)* ~**ly** li
  ~**ness** nəs nɪs

Secondary + primary stress

When the primary stress in longer words occurs late in the word, there is a secondary stress on the first or second syllable.

ˌsuperˈsonic

secondary stress   primary stress

EXERCISE 46

AIM: TO RECOGNISE SECONDARY AND PRIMARY STRESS WHEN YOU HEAR A WORD.
TO MARK SECONDARY AND PRIMARY STRESS.

Listen to these words on the cassette. Mark the secondary and primary stress, as in the example on page 43.

1. **anniversary**   6. **mortification**

2. **definition**   7. **proclamation**

3. **epicurean**   8. **regeneration**

4. **mediocrity**   9. **valediction**

5. **metaphysical**

Use the words above to fill the gaps below. Say the titles.

The .... *Poets*

A selection of poems

.... *in love rejected*	Thomas Carew
A ....; *forbidding mourning*	John Donne
The	John Donne
An Ode upon his Majestie's	Sir Richard Fanshawe
An .... *Ode*	John Hall
....	George Herbert
The .... *of Love*	Andrew Marvell
....	Henry Vaughan

EXERCISE 47
AIM: TO MARK SECONDARY AND PRIMARY STRESS.

The following words each have two stressed syllables, with the later stressed syllable carrying the primary stress. Mark the two stressed syllables. You can look the words up in the dictionary to check. The first one is done for you.

1. ˌsabbaˈtarian
2. sacramental
3. sacrificial
4. sacrilegious

5. Sagittarius
6. Salamanca
7. Salieri
8. salmonella

Some words have a secondary stress marked in brackets
   e.g. ₍ₗ₎San ˈRemo
This means that some speakers put a secondary stress on the first syllable:
   ˌSan ˈRemo
and others do not stress it:
   San ˈRemo

Tertiary stress – after primary stress

In multi-syllabic words, there is sometimes a rhythmic beat on a syllable after the primary stress. This syllable is not usually accented when the word is in a sentence. It is marked   and referred to as tertiary stress.

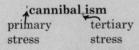

ˈcannibalˌism
primary   tertiary
stress   stress

EXERCISE 48

AIM: TO RECOGNISE TERTIARY STRESS AFTER THE PRIMARY STRESS WHEN YOU HEAR A WORD.
TO MARK PRIMARY AND TERTIARY STRESS.

Listen to the following words and phrases on the cassette. Each has two stressed syllables, with the earlier stressed syllable carrying the primary stress. Mark the stressed syllables, as in the example on page 45. The first one is done for you.

1. 'rain₀forest
2. octosyllable
3. revisionism
4. caretaker
5. castaway
6. undercarriage
7. upbringing

8. obstructionism
9. officeholder
10. estate agent
11. record library
12. Oedipus complex
13. uncertainty principle

EXERCISE 49

AIM: TO DISTINGUISH BETWEEN: PRIMARY STRESS + TERTIARY STRESS e.g. 'super₀market
SECONDARY STRESS + PRIMARY STRESS e.g. ,super'sonic

Look up the following items in the dictionary and check the stress. Mark the stress.

1. safebreaker
2. safe-conduct
3. safe-deposit

4. safekeeping
5. safety curtain
6. safety-first

Tertiary stress – between secondary and primary stress

There is another context in which tertiary stress occurs. Words with secondary and primary stress sometimes have a rhythmic beat between the secondary and primary stress. This is marked   and referred to as tertiary stress.

,inde₀fensi'bility

secondary + tertiary + primary stress

46

EXERCISE 50

AIM: TO RECOGNISE PRIMARY, SECONDARY AND TERTIARY STRESS WHEN YOU HEAR WORDS.
TO MARK PRIMARY, SECONDARY AND TERTIARY STRESS.

Listen to the following words and phrases on the cassette. Each has three stressed syllables, with the last stressed syllable carrying the primary stress. Mark the secondary, tertiary and primary stress in these words and phrases. The first one is done for you.

1. ˌcoˏeduˈcation
2. intercontinental
3. sadomasochistic
4. valetudinarian
5. Received pronunciation
6. co-efficient of friction
7. occupational therapy

EXERCISE 51

AIM: TO RECOGNISE STRESS PATTERNS OF WORDS WHEN YOU HEAR THEM (MIXED PATTERNS).

Listen to the following words on the cassette. Mark the stress.

1. tyrannicide
2. indivisibility
3. sacrificial
4. caretaker
5. liberator
6. adolescence
7. sacrosanct
8. intellectual
9. unconventionality
10. capitalism

EXERCISE 52

AIM: TO USE THE DICTIONARY TO CHECK STRESS PATTERNS.

a. Mark what you think is the stress pattern on the following words.
b. Then look each word up, and check if your stress marking is correct. Write the correct stress marking, if necessary.

Your stress marking	Correct stress marking
1. habilitate	habilitate
2. habilitation	habilitation
3. habit	habit
4. habitability	habitability
5. habitat	habitat
6. habitation	habitation
7. habit-forming	habit-forming

EXERCISE 53

AIM: TO USE THE DICTIONARY TO CHECK STRESS PATTERNS.

a. Mark what you think is the stress pattern on the following words.

b. Then look each word up, and check if your stress marking is correct. Write the correct stress marking, if necessary.

Your stress marking	Correct stress marking
1. daredevil	daredevil
2. deactivate	deactivate
3. deputation	deputation
4. deputy	deputy
5. deregulation	deregulation
6. derelict	derelict
7. dermatitis	dermatitis
8. derogatory	derogatory
9. desecrate	desecrate
10. discrimination	discrimination
11. dishonest	dishonest
12. dishwater	dishwater

10 Stress shift

Some words seem to change their stress pattern in connected speech; the position of the stress is shifted when the word is followed in a phrase by a more strongly stressed word. Words which are likely to undergo stress shift are marked ◄ in the dictionary.

> **middle-aged** ˌmɪd ᵊl ˈeɪdʒd ◄
> ˌmiddle-aged ˈspread

This means that in isolation, **middle-aged** has primary stress on 'aged'. So in the sentence:

Most Daily Telegraph readers are middle-aged.

'aged' is more prominent than 'middle'.
But in the phrase **middle-aged spread**, with primary stress on the noun 'spread', it is 'middle' and not 'aged' that carries the secondary stress: i.e. 'middle' is more prominent than 'aged'.

EXERCISES 54–58
AIM: TO RECOGNISE, MARK AND PRONOUNCE WORDS WHICH UNDERGO STRESS SHIFT.

EXERCISE 54

Listen to the example on the cassette. Notice the stress shift.

arrangements made at the last minute
last minute arrangements

The phrases below can all be transformed in a similar way. Transform each phrase. Mark the secondary and primary stress. The first one is done for you.

1. arrangements made at the last minute ˌlast-minute arˈrangements

2. a map drawn to a large scale

3. surgery performed on the open heart

4. a personality which is laid-back

5. a potato-peeler designed for people who are left-handed

6. a letter which is misspelt

7. a person's youth which was misspent

EXERCISE 55

In words of four or more syllables, when stress is shifted, the original primary stress still carries a rhythmic beat; this tertiary stress is marked ˌ.

e.g. atmospheric   atmospheric pressure
    ˌæt məs 'fer ɪk   ˌæt məs ˌfer ɪk 'preʃ ə

A similar process may take place in the words and phrases below. Say and mark the stress in the word in isolation, and the phrase containing the word:

1a. **audio-visual**   b. audio-visual aids

2a. **automatic**   b. automatic pilot

3a. **occupational**   b. occupational therapy

4a. **operational**   b. operational research

5a. **radioactive**   b. radioactive decay

EXERCISE 56

The phrases below are all given in the dictionary as examples of a phrase in which the first element is likely to undergo stress shift. Each phrase could be expressed in a longer form, with a relative clause:

e.g. next-door neighbours = neighbours who live next door.

Listen to the example on the cassette, and notice the difference in stress when 'next-door' is in final position:

ˌnext-door 'neighbours = neighbours who live ˌnext 'door

Express each of the phrases below in a similar way. When you say the two versions, be careful to stress correctly the element in final position.

1. trumped-up charges   *charges which are trumped up*

2. the mid-day sun

3. an undercover agent

4. unearned income

5. a middle-aged man

6. cast-iron railings

7. a crazy mixed-up kid

EXERCISE 57

Say the following pairs of sentences.

1. Don't go out at mid-day.
   Don't go out in the mid-day sun.

2. She's always at my right-hand.
   She's always on the right-hand side.

3. They're soft-hearted.
   They're a soft-hearted couple.

4. I'm going via Panama.
   I'm going via the Panama Canal.

5. She was sent overseas.
   She was sent on an overseas posting.

6. John's at university.
   John's at University College.

7. They're cruising in the Adriatic.
   They're cruising in the Adriatic Sea.

8. He's very interested in Latin America.
   He's very interested in Latin-American dancing.

9. The underlying rocks are carboniferous.
   The underlying rocks are carboniferous limestone.

10. We're going to Oklahoma.
    We're going to Oklahoma City.

EXERCISE 58

Continue this description of a book, using as many as possible of the words and phrases in Exercises 54 to 57. Compare your version with somebody else's, or record yourself reading it aloud.

11 Compounds and phrases

Early and late stress

There are many English expressions consisting of two words, or in which two words have been combined.

   e.g. **central heating**   **picture frame**   **dishwasher**

Some of these have early stress: primary stress is on the *first* element.

   e.g. **'picture frame**   **'dishwasher**

Some have late stress: primary stress is on the *second* element.

   e.g. **,central 'heating**

Can you give any guidelines for the placement of the stress? Write down what you think before you turn over the page.

Early and late stress: some guidelines

Early stress is usual in:

Compounds in which the two elements are written as one word,
e.g. 'dishwasher, 'blackbird

Expressions consisting of NOUN + NOUN,
e.g. 'picture frame

Late stress is usual in:

Expressions consisting of ADJECTIVE + NOUN,
e.g. ,central 'heating

Note that a word ending in -ing may operate as a noun
e.g. a 'washing ma₀chine (a machine for doing the washing)
     a 'swimming ₀lesson (a lesson in swimming)
OR a present participle, with the force of:
an adjective e.g.   a ,moving 'story (a story which is moving,
                    emotional)
a verb e.g.   ,moving 'pictures (pictures which move:
                    hence 'movies')

EXERCISES 59–62

AIM: TO UNDERSTAND AND USE GUIDELINES FOR PREDICTING STRESS IN COMPOUNDS AND PHRASES.

EXERCISE 59

For each of the expressions underlined in the following text, decide whether it has early or late stress. Write it in the correct column of the table below. The first one is done for you.

> I am taking Spanish lessons at the moment. I attend evening classes on Monday evenings at the local Community Centre. We've got an English teacher, and of course her Spanish accent isn't perfect, but she understands the problems we have, and we are making progress. Some of us have formed our own study group, and we meet during the week to practise. One of the members is a civil engineer whose driving ambition is to go to South America. Another is a driving instructor, who keeps his grammar book in the car so he can study between lessons. Occasionally he forgets, and amazes his pupils by giving directions in Spanish.

Early stress e.g. 'picture frame	Late stress e.g. ˌcentral 'heating
Spanish lessons	Monday evenings

The text is recorded on the cassette so you can listen to check your answers, before you compare your version with the key.

EXERCISE 60

Notice the difference in stress:

   a 'blackbird = a kind of bird: *Turdus merula*
   a ˌblack 'bird = any bird which is black

Using this pattern, what would you call the things defined below? Write the words and mark the stress.

1a. .... = a teacher of English

 b. .... = a teacher who is English

2a. .... = a lightless room for developing photographs

 b. .... = a room with not much light in it

3a. .... = a board with a specially treated black surface, traditionally used in classrooms for writing on with chalk

 b. .... = a board painted black

4a. .... = a shelf for keeping glasses on

 b. .... = a shelf made of glass

Some expressions, which are grammatically compounds, are nevertheless pronounced with late stress (= as if they were phrases). There is no firm rule; that is why many compounds and phrases are listed separately in LPD with their stress patterns.

One group of expressions of this type comprises those where the first element names the **material or ingredient** out of which a thing is made.

    a ˌrubber 'duck
    ˌpaper 'plates
    ˌcheese 'sandwiches
    ˌapple 'crumble
    a ˌpork 'pie

Note, however, that expressions involving **cake, juice, water** take early stress.

    'almond cake
    'orange juice
    'barley ˌwater   LPD note: COMPOUNDS & PHRASES: 5

EXERCISE 61

KEY

The following items can be divided into two groups. Write each item in the correct group.

apple blossom
apple pie
cheese grater
cheese sauce
jam jar
jam sandwich
peach brandy
peach stone
rubber duck
rubber plant
salt beef
salt cellar

Late stress
rubber duck

Early stress
rubber plant

In names of thoroughfares, note that all take late stress except **street**, which takes early stress.

ˌMelrose ˈRoad
ˌLavender ˈCrescent
ˌOxford ˈCircus
ˌKing's ˈAvenue
but ˈGower Street   LPD note: COMPOUNDS & PHRASES: 6

EXERCISE 62

Below is a list of places which a visitor to London might wish to visit, together with the name of the nearest Underground station.

a. Mark the stress in the names of the stations. The first one is done for you.

b. Using the underground map, plan a route, visiting all the places listed, in the most efficient order. Compare your route with someone else's, or record yourself describing your route; make sure you stress the stations correctly.

	Nearest Underground Station
Tower of London	ˌTower 'Hill
National Gallery	Charing Cross
Harrods	Knightsbridge
West End cinemas & theatres	Leicester Square
Madame Tussaud's	Baker Street
Statue of Eros	Piccadilly Circus
Speakers' Corner	Marble Arch
Barbican Centre	Moorgate
British Museum	Tottenham Court Road
shopping	Bond Street, Oxford Circus

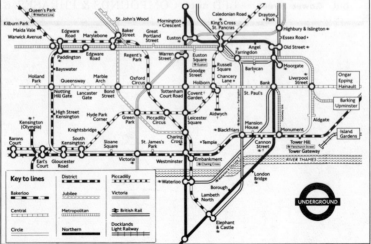

LRT Registered User No. 90/1254

58

The general guidelines on page 52 are very useful, but they do not give a firm rule for all expressions. That is why many expressions are listed in the dictionary.

EXERCISE 63
AIM: TO USE THE DICTIONARY TO CHECK THE STRESS PATTERN OF COMPOUNDS.

a. Mark what you think is the stress pattern in the following compounds.
b. Then look up each compound, and check if your stress marking is correct. Write the correct stress marking, if necessary.

Your stress marking	Correct stress marking
1. takeaway	takeaway
2. talcum powder	talcum powder
3. tank engine	tank engine
4. tonic water	tonic water
5. top drawer	top drawer
6. touch-type	touch-type
7. totem-pole	totem-pole
8. trapdoor	trapdoor
9. tumbleweed	tumbleweed
10. tumble-drier	tumble-drier
11. tunnel vision	tunnel vision
12. typewriter	typewriter

12 Alternative pronunciations with different stress

Some words have alternative pronunciations which differ from the main pronunciation only in their stress. The alternative stress pattern is shown using blocks to represent syllables.
e.g.

> **codriver** ˈkəʊ ˌdraɪv ə ˌ·'··

(The blocks stand for: ˌkəʊˈdraɪv ə)

EXERCISES 64–66

AIM: TO UNDERSTAND THE CONVENTIONS USED TO SHOW ALTERNATIVE PRONUNCIATIONS WITH DIFFERENT STRESS. TO IDENTIFY ALTERNATIVE PRONUNCIATIONS WHEN YOU HEAR THEM.

EXERCISE 64

a. Look at the dictionary entries shown below. Listen to the cassette. For each word, the main and alternative pronunciations are given.

1. **absolute** ˈæb sə luːt ˌ··'·

2. **backgammon** ˈbæk ˌgæm ən ·'··

3. **backpedal, back-pedal** ˌbæk ˈped əl '·ˌ··

4. **caviar, caviare** ˈkæv i ɑː ˌ··'·

5. **cigarette** ˌsɪg ə ˈret '···

6. **manageress** ˌmæn ɪdʒ ə ˈres '····

7. **submarine** n, adj ˈsʌb mə riːn ˌ··'·

8. **ˌAdam's ˈapple** ‖ '··ˌ··

9. **ˌice ˈcream,** '··

10. **ˌradio aˈlarm,** '···ˌ·

b. Listen to the words on the cassette. For each word, circle the appropriate stress pattern shown in a. above.

EXERCISE 65

The words and phrases below all have an alternative stress pattern given in the dictionary

a. Mark what you think are the main and alternative stress patterns. The first one is done for you.

1. value added tax ˌ···ₒ··ˈ·
8. violin ···

2. vaseline ···
9. violinist ····

3. velveteen ···
10. Virgin Islands ····

4. verifiable ·····
11. vivisect ···

5. vicereine ··
12. vocal cords ···

6. video cassette ·····
13. voiceover ···

7. video cassette recorder ········
14. Voltaire ··

b. Look up the words in the dictionary to check. Correct your marking if necessary.

c. Listen to the sentences below, on the cassette. For each of the words or phrases underlined, identify whether the stress pattern used is that of the main pronunciation or the alternative. Circle the correct letter – M for main, or A for alternative. The first one is done for you.

⊛/A   M/A
1. Is value added tax charged on video-cassettes?
        M/A   M/A
2. My neighbour is a violinist. She plays a violin made in the
    M/A
    Virgin Islands.

3. Old leather books can be preserved by treating the surface
        M/A   M/A
    with vaseline, and wrapping them in velveteen.
                                             M/A
4. I was once offered a job doing a voiceover for a television
    advertisement. The pay was marvellous, but I developed an
                           M/A
    infection of the vocal cords and couldn't do it.

5. 'Who said that the only meaningful statements are those
                M/A
    which are verifiable by sense experience?' 'It sounds like
    M/A
    Voltaire.'

61

Some words have alternative pronunciations involving differences in both stress and sounds.

Consider a word with an unstressed syllable containing a weak vowel e.g. the first syllable of **applicable** ə 'plɪk ə bᵊl

An alternative pronunciation which <u>stresses</u> the first syllable will contain a strong vowel instead of the weak vowel:
'æp lɪk ə bᵊl

EXERCISE 66

a. Can you give two pronunciations of the following words? Say and write what you think.

1. **harass** 'hær əs həˈræs

2. **brochure** ....

3. **clandestine** ....

4. **communal** ....

5. **contribute** ....

6. **controversy** ....

7. **decade** ....

8. **kilometre** ....

9. **primarily** ....

10. **subsidence** ....

b. Look up the words in the dictionary to check. Notice the stressed syllables and the vowels which are different. Correct your versions, if necessary. Notice which is the main pronunciation.

c. Listen to four sentences, which include the words below, on the cassette. For each word, transcribe the pronunciation you hear, and say whether it is given in the dictionary as the main (M) or alternative (A) pronunciation. The first one is done for you.

1. **brochure** 'brəʊʃ ə M

2. **applicable** ....

3. **primarily** ....

4. **subsidence** ....

5. **decade** ....

6. **communal** ....

7. **harass** ....

8. **controversy** ....

9. **clandestine** ....

10. **contributed** ....

13 Suffixes

EXERCISE 67
AIM: TO CONSIDER STRESS IN WORDS WITH SUFFIXES.

KEY a. Add a suffix to each of the words below to form an abstract noun. Mark the stress in the original word and the related noun. Does the stress change when the suffix is added? Write 'Yes' if it does, and 'No' if it doesn't.

1. 'regular   ˌregu'larity   Yes
2. inform
3. entertain
4. electric
5. careless

KEY b. Add a suffix to each of the words below to form an adjective. Mark the stress in the original word and the related adjective. Does the stress change when the suffix is added?

1. plenty
2. photograph
3. beauty
4. value
5. Japan

c. Look at the words in a. and b. where the stress changes with the addition of a suffix. You will see that in some cases, the stress falls on the suffix; in others, it has moved to a different syllable of the stem.

We can identify three types of suffix, from the point of view of stress:

Stress-neutral suffix – the suffix does not affect the location of stress in the stem to which it is attached.
   e.g. -ful   'beauty   'beautiful

Stress-imposing suffix – the suffix causes the stress to fall on a particular syllable of the stem.
   e.g. -ion: stress always falls on the syllable before the suffix
      'fashion   e'motion   ˌinfor'mation

Stressed suffix – the suffix itself is stressed.
   e.g. -ese   ˌJapan'ese

EXERCISE 68
AIM: TO IDENTIFY TYPES OF SUFFIX.

a. Each of the groups of words below contains:
1. a stress-neutral suffix SN
2. a stress-imposing suffix SI
3. a stressed suffix S
But they are not in the same order in every group.
In each group, mark which words contain which type of suffix.
The first one is done for you.

	'climate	cli'matic **2. SI**
A.	'Portugal	ˌPortu'guese **3. S**
	'poison	'poisonous **1. SN**

	launder	launderette
B.	comfort	comfortable
	period	periodical

	punctual	punctuality
C.	wide	widen
	mountain	mountaineer

	cigar	cigarette
D.	economy	economic
	sympathy	sympathise

	punish	punishment
E.	picture	picturesque
	proverb	proverbial

KEY

b. Use the suffixes in the words in a. to complete the table below, writing suffixes into the correct column. The first three are done for you.

Stress-neutral	Stress-imposing	Stressed
-ous	-ic	-ese

Dictionary entries for suffixes show which type of suffix they are, with an example.

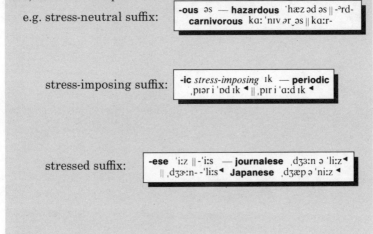

e.g. stress-neutral suffix:

-ous əs — **hazardous** ˈhæz əd əs ‖ -ᵊrd-
carnivorous kɑː ˈnɪv ər_əs ‖ kɑːr-

stress-imposing suffix:

-ic *stress-imposing* ɪk — **periodic**
ˌpɪər i ˈɒd ɪk ◀ ‖ ˌpɪr i ˈɑːd ɪk ◀

stressed suffix:

-ese ˈiːz ‖ -ˈiːs — **journalese** ˌdʒɜːn ə ˈliːz ◀
‖ ˌdʒɝːn- -ˈliːs ◀ **Japanese** ˌdʒæp ə ˈniːz ◀

EXERCISE 69

AIM: TO REMEMBER HOW SUFFIXES AFFECT STRESS.

a. Make up sentences or little texts using the words in exercise 68, and other words with these suffixes.

e.g. I <u>sympathise</u> with <u>mountaineers</u> who meet with terrible <u>climatic</u> <u>conditions</u>.

Record yourself saying the sentences, with the correct stress. Use the sentences for reference.

b. As you come across other suffixes, use the table in exercise 68 b. to keep a record of them. Make up sentences for those suffixes too.

C ASPECTS OF PRONUNCIATION IN THE DICTIONARY

14 American pronunciation

> **2.3 American pronunciation.** The AmE pronunciations shown in LPD are those appropriate to the variety (accent) known as **General American**. This is what is spoken by the majority of Americans, namely those who do not have a noticeable eastern or southern accent. It is the appropriate pronunciation for EFL learners who take AmE as their model, rather than BrE.

American pronunciation is discussed further in LPD INTRODUCTION 2.3, 3.1 and 3.2.

EXERCISES 70–75
AIM: TO BE ABLE TO PREDICT SOME DIFFERENCES IN PRONUNCIATION BETWEEN RP AND GenAm.

Some differences between RP and GenAm:
1. In GenAm, where there is an r in the spelling, it is always pronounced:

> **bird, Bird** bɜːd ‖ bɝːd

> **cart** kɑːt ‖ kɑːrt

> **teacher, T~** 'tiːtʃ ə ‖ -ᵊr

EXERCISE 70

KEY

Give the American pronunciations of the following words:

1. **stir** ....
2. **third** ....
3. **leader** ....
4. **larger** ....
5. **barn** ....

2. In some words such as 'fast', where RP has ɑː, GenAm (like northern English accents) has æ.

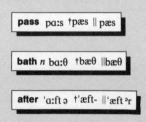

pass pɑːs †pæs ‖ pæs

bath *n* bɑːθ †bæθ ‖bæθ

after ˈɑːft ə †ˈæft- ‖ˈæft ᵊr

EXERCISE 71

Give the American pronunciations of the following words:

1. **craft** ....
2. **flask** ....
3. **laughter** ....
4. **banana** ....
5. **past** ....

Notice that not all RP ɑː sounds are pronounced æ in GenAm:

fath|er ˈfɑːð |ə ‖ -|ᵊr

3. The distribution of back vowels is different. Compare:

RP

ɒ	**lot odd**
ɔː	**thought law north war**
ɑː	**start father**

GenAm (Note that there is considerable variation among speakers of General American, and not all speakers make all the following distinctions.)

ɑː	**lot odd start father**
ɒː	**thought law** (if not ɑː)
ɔː	**north war**
oː	*variant of* ɔː *in* **force, four**

EXERCISE 72

What vowel is used in the following words, in RP and in GenAm?
Write each word alongside the correct vowel below, for RP and
for GenAm.

card   cord   harm   lawn   thorn   wrong

RP

1. ɒ ....

2. ɔː ....

3. ɑː ....

GenAm

4. ɑː ....

5. ɒː ....

6. ɔː ....

---

4. For most Americans, ə and ɪ are not distinct as weak vowels
(so that **rabbit** rhymes with **abbot**). For American
pronunciation, LPD follows the rule of showing ɪ before
palato-alveolar and velar consonants (ʃ tʃ ʒ dʒ k g ŋ), and in
prefixes such as **re-**, **e-**, **de-**; but ə elsewhere. Where no
separate indication is given for the American
pronunciation, it may be assumed that it has ə or ɪ
according to this rule.

LPD INTRODUCTION 2.3

EXERCISE 73

Which weak vowel, ə or ɪ, is used in American pronunciation in
the unstressed syllable of the following words? Write the correct
vowel. The first two are done for you.

1. cabʙage   3. **habit**   5. **Lenin**   7. **vanish**   9. **carriage**
    ɪ

2. **robin**   4. **panic**   6. **wicked**   8. **arches**
  ə

5. The RP diphthongs ɪə, eə are replaced in GenAm by pure vowels.

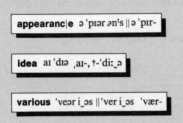

appearanc|e ə 'pɪər ən's ‖ ə 'pɪr-

idea aɪ 'dɪə ˌaɪ-, †-'diːˌə

various 'veər i‿əs ‖ 'ver i‿əs 'vær-

In some words, some American speakers do include ə before r; this is shown in the dictionary by ᵊ.

pier pɪə ‖ pɪᵊr

pear peə ‖ peᵊr pæᵊr

EXERCISE 74

KEY a. Transcribe the RP and GenAm pronunciations of the following words.

	RP	GenAm
1. **staring**		
2. **careful**		
3. **dearest**		
4. **experience**		
5. **variation**		
6. **sincerely**		

KEY b. Listen to the words on the cassette. For each one, circle the appropriate pronunciation (RP or GenAm) in a. above.

6. T-voicing
In GenAm, t can be voiced when it occurs between vowels, at the end of a syllable e.g. **shutter** 'ʃʌ̬t ᵊr. It may sound identical with d e.g. **shudder** 'ʃʌd ᵊr.
(For a fuller account, see LPD note: T-VOICING.)

EXERCISE 75

KEY

In which of these words would the t be voiced in GenAm? Circle the voiced t's. The first one is done for you.

1. wri(t)ing   3. return   5. softer   7. attack
2. later   4. related   6. attic   8. lightning

EXERCISES 76–77
QUIZZES ON AMERICAN PRONUNCIATIONS.

EXERCISE 76
ODD ONE OUT.

Consider the GenAm vowel sound in the stressed syllable in the following groups of words. In each group, one word has a different vowel sound in GenAm from the others. Circle the odd

KEY

one out.

1. rafter   rather   rock   rod
2. after   class   father   ghastly
3. sordid   worthy   warden   warm

EXERCISE 77
RHYMES QUIZ.

There once was an old English Lord
Whose views were exceedingly broad.
He said: 'I don't worry
How people say "furry".'
That tolerant old English Lord.

In the following words, find three pairs which rhyme in RP but not in GenAm, and three pairs which can rhyme in GenAm but

KEY

not in RP. Fill in the table.

**abbot bother clerk court father habit laugh
mark nought scarf sorry story**

RP rhymes	GenAm rhymes

EXERCISE 78
AIM: TO STUDY THE FEATURES OF AMERICAN PRONUNCIATION IN A SPOKEN TEXT.

The text below is recorded on the cassette, by an American speaker.

Either: Listen to the cassette and transcribe the text. Use the key to check your transcription.

Or: Transcribe the text as you expect it to be spoken by an American speaker. Then listen to the cassette and/or look at the key and compare what you have written.

The car was a dark blue seven-passenger sedan, a Packard of the latest model, custom-built. It was the kind of car you wear your rope pearls in. It was parked by a fire-hydrant and a dark foreign-looking chauffeur with a face of carved wood was behind the wheel. The interior was upholstered in quilted grey chenille. The Indian put me in the back. Sitting there alone I felt like a high-class corpse, laid out by an undertaker with a lot of good taste.

The Indian got in beside the chauffeur and the car turned in the middle of the block and a cop across the street said: 'Hey,' weakly, as if he didn't mean it, and then bent down quickly to tie his shoe.

We went west, dropped over to Sunset and slid fast and noiseless along that. The Indian sat motionless beside the chauffeur. An occasional whiff of his personality drifted back to me. The driver looked as if he was half asleep but he passed the fast boys in the convertible sedans as though they were being towed. They turned on all the green lights for him. Some drivers are like that. He never missed one.

It had been a warm afternoon, but the heat was gone. We whipped past a distant cluster of lighted buildings and an endless series of lighted mansions, not too close to the road. We dipped down to skirt a huge green polo field with another equally huge practice field beside it, soared again to the top of a hill and swung mountainward up a steep hill road of clean concrete that passed orange groves, some rich man's pet because this is not orange country, and then little by little the lighted windows of the millionaires' homes were gone and the road narrowed and this was Stillwood Heights.

Farewell, My Lovely Raymond Chandler (Penguin edition p.126)

15 Homophones

A number of dictionary entries show a homophone – another word, with a different spelling, which has the same pronunciation.

write raɪt *(= right)*

bear *n, v* beə ‖beᵊr bæᵊr *(= bare)*

EXERCISE 79

AIM: TO USE THE DICTIONARY MARKING OF HOMOPHONES AS A QUICK WAY OF CHECKING WHETHER PAIRS OF WORDS HAVE THE SAME PRONUNCIATION.

In the sentences below, some of the pairs of words underlined have the same pronunciation, and some have different pronunciations. You can check quickly by looking up the first underlined word in each pair. Mark whether the pronunciations are the same (S) or different (D).

1. The government annalist got so depressed studying the annals that he had to go to an analyst for treatment.   .S.
2. A Victorian lady who sat in her parlour and shunned the sun took pride in the pallor of her cheeks.   ....
3. I've been on a cruise several times, and the crews have all been very efficient.   ....
4. They leant on the door so that their sister couldn't go out until she lent them some money.   ....
5. The weather which has been becalming the sailing boats is becoming better.   ....
6. The baron ruled over hundreds of acres of barren land.   ....
7. The assistant who packed the box left out this packet.   ....
8. If the clasp of your brooch is too loose, you could easily lose it.   ....
9. There are ten canons at Westchester Cathedral, and ten cannons at Westchester Castle.   ....
10. A teacher wouldn't lessen my interest in the subject by giving one tedious lesson.   ....

16 Abbreviations

Some abbreviations consisting of the initial letters of words are acronyms – the letters are pronounced as if they are a word:

e.g. **SALT** sɔːlt sɒlt ‖ sɒːlt sɑːlt
(Strategic Arms Limitation Talks)

In others, the letters are pronounced separately:

e.g. **VIP** ˌviː aɪ ˈpiː (very important person)

Some abbreviations are pronounced in both ways:

e.g. **VAT** ˌviː eɪ ˈtiː væt (value added tax)

EXERCISE 80

AIM: TO USE THE DICTIONARY TO CHECK THE PRONUNCIATION OF ABBREVIATIONS.

KEY

The following items are all commonly abbreviated. Use the dictionary to check whether the initial letters are pronounced as an acronym or separately; enter the abbreviation in the correct column. The first two are done for you.

	Acronym	Separate letters
1. General Certificate of Secondary Education		GCSE
2. General Agreement on Tariffs and Trade	GATT gæt	
3. Organisation for Economic Co-operation and Development		
4. Organisation of Petroleum Exporting Countries		
5. Trades Union Congress		
6. Universities Central Council on Admissions		
7. University of California at Los Angeles.		
8. unilateral declaration of independence		
9. United Nations Educational, Scientific and Cultural Organisation		

17 Names of people and places

Slough

Come, friendly bombs, and fall on Slough
It isn't fit for humans now,
There isn't grass to graze a cow
Swarm over, Death!

The town satirised in John Betjeman's poem, and the English county in which it is situated, Berkshire, both have pronunciations which are difficult to predict from their spelling. The dictionary contains a large number of names – English names that may present a problem, the English pronunciation of English names which are commonly used in other languages, the English pronunciation of foreign names.

EXERCISE 81
QUIZ.

Use the dictionary to help you answer the questions.

1. **Renault** cars are French – how are they pronounced in England, and in the USA?
2. **Frances** is a woman's name: **Francis** is a man's name and a surname. Is the pronunciation the same or different?
3. **Eau-de-cologne** means literally 'water from **Cologne**' – but is **cologne** pronounced the same way?
4. The University of Essex is at **Norwich**; the University of Kent is at **Canterbury**, and the nearest town to the University of Sussex is **Lewes**. How are the three places pronounced?
5. **Birmingham**, England, and **Birmingham**, Alabama, USA – same or different?
6. **Olive's olives**: – same or different?
7. 'When I tell English people I come from Valencia, they don't understand me.' How do they pronounce **Valencia**?
8. Sir Peter **Pears**, the singer, and **Pears** soap – same or different?
9. **London**: 'lʌnd n or 'lʌnd ən?
10. Edward **Lear**, the poet, and Shakespeare's King **Lear** – same or different?

11. 'Yes. I remember **Adlestrop**'
    'I will arise and go now, and go to **Innisfree**'
    '**Albion's** most lovely daughter sat on the banks of the
    Mersey dangling her landing stage in the water'
    These are the first lines of poems by **Edward Thomas, W B
    Yeats**, and **Adrian Henri** respectively. How are the places,
    and the poets, pronounced?

18 Assimilation

1 **Assimilation** is a type of COARTICULATION. It is the alteration of a speech sound to make it more similar to its neighbours.

2 The alveolar consonants t,d,n, when they occur at the end of a word or syllable, can optionally assimilate to the place of articulation of the consonant at the beginning of the next syllable.
Thus n can become m before p,b,m, as in the examples

    ten men ˌten ˈmen → ˌtem ˈmen
    downbeat ˈdaʊn biːt → ˈdaʊm biːt

Similarly, n can become ŋ before k,g, as in:

    fine grade ˌfaɪn ˈgreɪd → ˌfaɪŋ ˈgreɪd
    incredible ɪn ˈkred əb ᵊl → ɪŋ ˈkred əb ᵊl

In the same way d can change to b and g respectively, as in

    red paint ˌred ˈpeɪnt → ˌreb ˈpeɪnt
    admit əd ˈmɪt → əb ˈmɪt
    bad guys ˈbæd gaɪz → ˈbæg gaɪz

It is also possible for t to change to p and k respectively, though a more frequent possibility is for t to be realized as a GLOTTAL STOP when followed by another consonant:

    eight boys ˌeɪt ˈbɔɪz → ˌeɪˀ ˈbɔɪz (ˌeɪp ˈbɔɪz)

Where dictionary entries contain alternative pronunciations which are derived by assimilation, they are preceded by →, the symbol for a pronunciation derived by rule.

EXERCISE 82
AIM: TO PREDICT ASSIMILATION OF ALVEOLAR CONSONANTS.

KEY

The following words, shown with their main pronunciation, all have an alternative derived by assimilation. Write the pronunciation with assimilation.

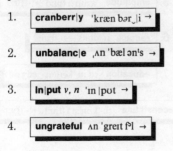

1. **cranberr|y** ˈkræn bər‿ji →

2. **unbalanc|e** ˌʌn ˈbæl ən's →

3. **in|put** v, n ˈɪn ǀpʊt →

4. **ungrateful** ʌn ˈgreɪt fᵊl →

5. **record-break|er/s** 'rek ɔːd ˌbreɪk |ə/z †-əd-, →

6. **midpoint** 'mɪd pɔɪnt →

7. **broadcast** 'brɔːd kɑːst →

8. **weedkiller** 'wiːd ˌkɪl ə →

---

5 **Yod coalescence** (or **coalescent assimilation**) is the process which changes t or d plus j into tʃ or dʒ respectively.

6 Within a word, the status of yod coalescence depends on whether the following vowel is strong or weak (see WEAK VOWELS).
—Where the vowel is strong, i.e. uː or ʊə, yod coalescence can frequently be heard in BrE, although it is not considered standard. (In AmE there is usually no j present, so the possibility of assimilation does not arise.)

tune tjuːn→ †tʃuːn
endure ɪn 'djʊə→ †ɪn 'dʒʊə
—Where the vowel is weak, i.e. u or ə, assimilation is usually variable in RP but obligatory in GenAm.

factual 'fækt ju ͜ əl→ 'fæk tʃu ͜ əl
educate 'ed ju keɪt -jə- → 'edʒ u keɪt -ə-

LPD note: ASSIMILATION 5 & 6

EXERCISE 83

AIM: TO IDENTIFY ASSIMILATION WHEN YOU HEAR WORDS CONTAINING t OR d BEFORE j.

Look at the dictionary entries below, and listen to the words on the cassette. For each entry, circle the pronunciation you hear. The first one is done for you.

1. **costume** *n, adj* 'kɒs tjuːm →⟨'kɒs tʃuːm⟩

2. **tube** tjuːb →†tʃuːb

3. **mildew** 'mɪl djuː →†-dʒuː

4. **adduc|e** ə 'djuːs →†-'dʒuːs

5. **amplitude** 'æmp lɪ tjuːd →†-tʃuːd

6. **reduc|e** rɪ 'djuːs →†-'dʒuːs

7. **education** ˌed ju 'keɪʃ ᵊn ˌedʒ u-

8. **reconsti|tute** ˌriː 'kɒnst ɪ |tjuːt →†- tʃuːt

EXERCISE 84

AIM: TO IDENTIFY ASSIMILATION WHEN YOU HEAR IT, INCLUDING ASSIMILATION OF FINAL CONSONANTS INFLUENCED BY THE FOLLOWING WORD.

The following text is recorded on the cassette. Use it as you wish. Three different approaches are suggested.

Suggestion 1. Listen to the cassette, and transcribe the text, paying particular attention to assimilation.

Suggestion 2. Read the text, and predict where assimilation might take place. Underline the sounds you predict. Then listen to the cassette and check how those sounds are pronounced.

Suggestion 3. Listen to the cassette with the text in front of you. Circle the words where you hear assimilation.

He swung round startled. *A knock on his door!* There must be some mistake. Or his ears were playing him tricks. The darkness of the room – for he had not yet switched on the lights – made this seem more plausible. But no – the knock was repeated.

'Come in,' he said in a thin, cracked voice, and cleared his throat. 'Come in!' He moved eagerly towards the door to welcome his visitor, and to turn the lights on at the same time, but collided with a chair and dropped his cigar, which rolled under the table. He dived after it as the door opened. A segment of light from the corridor fell across the floor, but did not reveal the hiding-place of the cigar. A woman's voice said uncertainly, 'Professor Zapp?'

'Yeah, come in. Would you switch the light on, please?'

The lights came on and he heard the woman gasp. 'Where are you?'

'Under here.' He found himself staring at a pair of thick fur-lined boots and the hemline of a shaggy fur coat. To these was added, a moment later, an inverted female face, scarved, red-nosed and apprehensive. 'I'll be right with you,' he said. 'I dropped my cigar somewhere under here.'

Changing Places David Lodge (Penguin edition pp. 83–84)

> Assimilation is also included in section 19, Pronunciations derived by rule, on pages 78–79. There is further discussion of assimilation in the note ASSIMILATION in LPD.

19 Pronunciations derived by rule

> The symbol → shows that an alternative pronunciation is the result of a general rule which affects not just this word but a whole range of words and phrases in the language. The dictionary only shows the results of such rules when they operate within the word, independently of surrounding words.

Examples:

question 'kwes tʃən →'kweʃ-,

Assimilation of the s, anticipating the following tʃ, produces 'kweʃ tʃən

newspaper 'njuːs ˌpeɪp ə

Assimilation: the z of njuːz is devoiced, anticipating the following unvoiced p. (This pronunciation is now standard).

handbag 'hænd bæg →'hæm-

Elision: 'hænd bæg becomes 'hæn bæg
+ assimilation: 'hæn bæg becomes 'hæm bæg

cold kəʊld →kɒʊld

Some varieties of RP use the special allophone ɒʊ before l in the same syllable.

includ|e ɪn 'kluːd →ɪŋ-

Anticipatory dealveolar assimilation of the n, anticipating the following k, produces ɪŋ 'kluːd

induc|e ɪn 'djuːs →t-'dʒuːs

Assimilation: coalescence of d and j to form dʒ.

EXERCISE 85

AIM: TO IDENTIFY RULES AFFECTING ALTERNATIVE PRONUNCIATIONS.

The dictionary entries below all include an alternative pronunciation derived by rule from the main pronunciation. In each case, state what rule is involved, as in the examples on page 80.

KEY

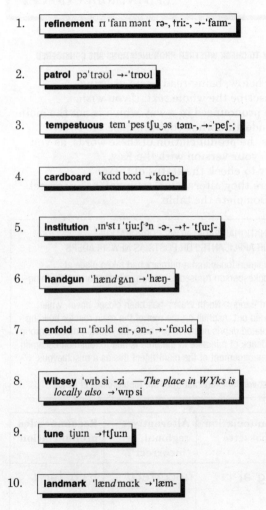

1. **refinement** rɪ'faɪn mənt rə-, †riː-, →-'faɪm-

2. **patrol** pə'trəʊl →-'trɒʊl

3. **tempestuous** tem'pes tʃu‿əs təm-, →-'peʃ-;

4. **cardboard** 'kɑːd bɔːd →'kɑːb-

5. **institution** ˌɪnˈstɪ 'tjuːʃ ᵊn -ə-, →†- 'tʃuːʃ-

6. **handgun** 'hænd gʌn →'hæŋ-

7. **enfold** ɪn 'fəʊld en-, ən-, →-'fɒʊld

8. **Wibsey** 'wɪb si -zi — *The place in WYks is locally also* →'wɪp si

9. **tune** tjuːn →†tʃuːn

10. **landmark** 'lænd mɑːk →'læm-

20 Incorrect pronunciations

—For a few words, LPD includes a pronunciation variant that is not considered standard. Although generally seen as incorrect, these variants are included because of the fact that they are in widespread use. They are marked with the special sign △.

LPD INTRODUCTION 2.2

EXERCISE 86

AIM: TO USE THE DICTIONARY TO CHECK WHETHER PRONUNCIATIONS ARE CONSIDERED INCORRECT.

a. Listen to the text below, being read by an aspiring newsreader. Transcribe the whole text, if you wish.

b. Twelve words are pronounced in a way which is not the main pronunciation. Underline what you think are the twelve words. Transcribe the pronunciation of these words, as you KEY heard it. Compare your version with the Key.

c. Use the dictionary to check the status of these pronunciations: are they alternative, regional, or 'incorrect' KEY pronunciations? Complete the table.

INTERNATIONAL RADIO NEWS CORPORATION
TEST PIECE FOR APPLICANTS FOR POSTS AS NEWSREADERS

Several London papers claimed today that a burglary had taken place at Buckingham Palace. A spokesperson refused to confirm whether or not anything had been stolen.

A nuclear power station in Bangor, North Wales, has been closed down, while maintenance work is carried out. Asphalt on the roof of the main reactor building has cracked, and accumulated debris needs to be removed. A local pressure group claim that increased incidence of migraine in the area is due to radiation escaping through the cracks. The management of the plant reject this as a mischievous attempt to cause alarm.

And now here is the latest weather forecast from the Meteorological Office . . .

Word	Pronunciation on cassette	Alternative, regional, or 'incorrect'?	Recommended pronunciation
burglary	bɜːg əl ri	incorrect	bɜːg lər i

21 Combining forms

1 Many learned words are composed of **combining forms** derived from Greek or Latin. These words consist of a first element and a second element. For example, **micro-** plus **-scopic** gives **microscopic**. LPD contains entries for these separate elements, which makes it possible to work out the pronunciation of many unlisted rare or new words.

2 Most combining form **suffixes** (= second elements) are **stress-neutral** (= they preserve the location of stresses in the first element). Others are **stress-imposing** (= they cause the main stress to fall on a particular syllable of the first element).

3 A first element usually has two different pronunciations, one used with stress-neutral suffixes, the other with stress-imposing suffixes. For the pronunciation of the whole word, the pronunciation for the suffix must be combined with the appropriate pronunciation for the first element.

4 The mark in the pronunciation of a first element means a stress. This will be a secondary stress ( ) if the suffix includes a main stress. If not, it will be a main stress (').

For example, take the first element **cata-**. With a stress-neutral suffix, it is pronounced ˌkæt ə Combining this with **-graphic** ˈgræf ɪk we get **catagraphic** ˌkæt ə ˈgræf ɪk Combining it with **-phyte** we get **cataphyte** ˈkæt ə faɪt

5 With a stress-imposing suffix, **cata-** is pronounced kə ˈtæ⁺. (The sign ⁺ is a reminder that this syllable is incomplete and must attract at least one consonant from the suffix.) Combining **cata-** with **-logy** lədʒi (stress-imposing), we get **catalogy** kə ˈtæl ədʒ i

The words **catagraphic, cataphyte, catalogy** probably do not exist. But an author could easily invent them. If they were to be used, this is how they would be pronounced.

EXERCISE 87
AIM: TO UNDERSTAND DICTIONARY ENTRIES ON COMBINING FORMS.

Study the entries below for first elements and suffixes.

First elements

Suffixes

caco- *comb. form*
  with stress-neutral suffix ˌkæk əʊ ‖ -ə —
  cacographic ˌkæk əʊ ˈgræf ɪk ◄ ‖ -ə-
  with stress-imposing suffix kæ ˈkɒ⁺ kə-
  ‖ kæ ˈkɑː⁺ — **cacography** kæ ˈkɒg rəf i
  kə- ‖ -ˈkɑːg-

-gamy *stress-imposing* gəm i

cardio- *comb. form*
  with stress-neutral suffix ˌkɑːd i ˌəʊ
  ‖ ˌkɑːrd i ˌoʊ ˌə — **cardiomyopathy**
  ˌkɑːd i ˌəʊ maɪ ˈɒp əθ i ‖ ˌkɑːrd i ˌoʊ maɪ ˈɑːp-
  with stress-imposing suffix ˌkɑːd i ˈɒ⁺
  ‖ ˌkɑːrd i ˈɑː⁺ — **cardiography**
  ˌkɑːd i ˈɒg rəf i‖ ˌkɑːrd i ˈɑːg-

-genous *stress-imposing* dʒən əs —

endo- *comb. form*
  with stress-neutral suffix ˌend əʊ ˌend ə
  — **endocranial** ˌend əʊ ˈkreɪn i ˌəl ◄ ‖ ˌ•ə-
  with stress-imposing suffix en ˈdɒ⁺
  ‖ en ˈdɑː⁺ — **endogenous** en ˈdɒdʒ ən əs
  -ɪn- ‖ -ˈdɑːdʒ-

-gram græm

mono- *comb. form*
  with stress-neutral suffix ˌmɒn əʊ ‖ˌmɑːn ə
  -oʊ , *but before a vowel always* -əʊ ‖ -oʊ
  — **monochord** ˈmɒn əʊ kɔːd
  ‖ˈmɑːn ə kɔːrd — **monoacidic**
  ˌmɒn əʊ ə ˈsɪd ɪk ◄ -æˈ•- ‖ˌmɑːn oʊ-
  with stress-imposing suffix mə ˈnɒ⁺ mɒ-
  ‖mə ˈnɑː⁺ mɑː- — **monology**
  mə ˈnɒl ədʒ i mɒ- ‖mə ˈnɑːl- mɑː-

-graphic ˈgræf ɪk

First elements

octa- *comb. form*
  with stress-neutral suffix ˌɒkt ə ‖ˌˈɑːkt ə —
  octachord ˈɒkt ə kɔːd ‖ ˈɑːkt ə kɔːrd
  with stress-imposing suffix ɒk ˈtæ⁺
  ‖ɑːk ˈtæ⁺ — **octameter** ɒk ˈtæm ɪt ə -ət-
  ‖ɑːk ˈtæm ət ᵊr

poly- *comb. form*
  with stress-neutral suffix ˌpɒl i ‖ˌˈpɑːl i
  —*but in certain more familiar words, before
  a consonant, also* ˌpɒl ə ‖ˌˈpɑːl ə —
  polygenesis ˌpɒl i ˈdʒen əs ɪs -ɪs ɪs, †- əs
  ‖ˌpɑːl-
  with stress-imposing suffix pə ˌˈlɪ⁺ pɒ- —
  polyphagous pə ˈlɪf əg əs pɒ-

Suffixes

-gonal *stress-imposing* gᵊn əl

-phony *stress-imposing* fən i

The following words combine elements shown above. Write the pronunciation of each word. (If you already know the pronunciation, look to see how the information is conveyed in the dictionary entries. If you are not sure of the pronunciation, work it out from the entries. Then you can check the transcription in the key, and listen to the pronunciations on the cassette.)

1. **cacophony** ....
2. **cardiographic** ....
3. **endogenous** ....
4. **monogram** ....
5. **octagonal** ....
6. **polygamy** ....

EXERCISE 88

AIM: TO USE DICTIONARY ENTRIES TO PREDICT PRONUNCIATION OF UNFAMILIAR WORDS.

Many other words can be formed by combining the elements shown in exercise 1. Some will be familiar, others will be unfamiliar either because you haven't met them before or because you have just created them. Devise ten words that are unfamiliar to you, and work out how they would be pronounced.

e.g. *endographic* ˌend əʊ ˈgræf ɪk

KEY

EXERCISE 1: a. 5 b. 12 c. 4 d. 17 e. 18 f. 20 g. 6 h. 3 i. 16
j. 13

EXERCISE 2: 1. creator 2. yet 7. below 8. surgeon 9. arrange
10. heart, hart 11. drug 14. avid 15. choice 19. wretched.

EXERCISE 3: 1. B ice 2. A ankle 3. B soul 4. A breathe 5. A avoid
6. B thing 7. B poses 8. B vine 9. A louvre 10. B feelings

EXERCISE 4: 1. A aɪz 2. B 'ʌŋkəl 3. A sɔɪl 4. B breθ 5. B ɪ 'veɪd
6. A θɪn 7. A pə 'zes 8. A veɪn 9. B 'lʌv ə 10. A 'fɪl ɪŋz

EXERCISE 5: 1. i 2. o 3. c 4. g 5. n 6. l 7. d 8. h

EXERCISE 6: a. leather b. washing e. catcher f. loose j. age
k. olive m. concord p. ledger

EXERCISE 7: 3D – but S in American 4S 5D 6D 7S 8D 9D 10S
11D 12D (but can be S in American)

EXERCISE 8: a. 19 b. 12 c. 4 d. 11 e. 2 f. 9 g. 6 h. 17 i. 15
j. 14

EXERCISE 9:

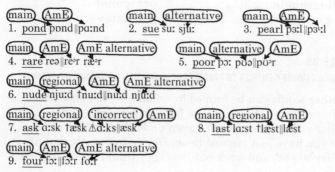

EXERCISE 10

	Main pron
1. match	mætʃ
2. ballad	'bæl əd
3. mead	miːd

	Main pron	Alternative pron
4. lewd	luːd	ljuːd
5. suit	suːt	sjuːt

	Main pron	AmE pron
6. mark	mɑːk	mɑːrk
7. dot	dɒt	dɑːt
8. herb	hɜːb	ɜˑb
9. part	pɑːt	pɑːrt

	Main pron	Regional pron	AmE pron
10. bath	bɑːθ	bæθ	bæθ
11. past	pɑːst	pæst	pæst

	Main pron	AmE pron	Alternative AmE pron
12. mayor	meə	meɪˌ°r	me°r
13. broad	brɔːd	brɒːd	brɑːd
14. ballet	'bæleɪ	bæ'leɪ	'bæleɪ
15. bare	beə	be°r	bæ°r

	Main pron	Regional pron	AmE pron	Alternative AmE pron
16. new	njuː	nuː	nuː	njuː
17. tube	tjuːb	tʃuːb	tuːb	tjuːb

EXERCISE 11

	Transcription	Which pron?	English or American?
Speaker 2:			
tour	tɔː	alternative	
part	pɑːt	main	English
poor	pɔː	main	
Speaker 3:			
rare	rær	AmE alternative	
new	nuː	AmE	
		– or regional	American
suit	suːt	main	
ballet	bæ 'leɪ	AmE	
Speaker 4:			
Tube	tʃuːb	regional	
last	læst	regional	English, with a
		– or AmE	regional accent
four	fɔː	main	

EXERCISE 12: 'Beautiful' – there are twelve pronunciations shown.

EXERCISE 16

2. opposite 'ɒp əz ɪt -ⓢ, †-ət‖ɑːp-   **'ɒp əs ɪt**

3. substantial ⓢəbstænⁱʃ ⓛtsʌb-, -ⓢtɑːnⁱʃ   **səb 'stɑːntʃ əl**

4. transistor træn ⓩɪst ətrɑːn-, ⓣtrən, -'sɪst-   **trən'zɪst ə**

5. decisive dɪ'saɪs ɪv ⓓə, †diː-, -ⓢaɪz   **də 'saɪz ɪv**

6. exasperate ɪg 'zæspⓐ reɪ eg-, əg-,ⓘk, ek-, ək-,ⓒ'zɑːsp ɪk **'zɑːsp ə reɪt**

EXERCISE 17

1. ˌæb ᵊr 'diːn

2. ə ˌkæd ə 'mɪʃ ᵊn, ˌæk əd ə 'mɪʃ ᵊn,
ə ˌkæd ɪ 'mɪʃ ᵊn, ˌæk əd ɪ 'mɪʃ ᵊn,
ə ˌkæd e 'mɪʃ ᵊn, ˌæk əd e 'mɪʃ ᵊn,

3. ˌæd ɪs 'æb əb ə

4. ˌmæn ədʒ ə 'res

5. ˌmɪs ˌrep riː zen 'teɪʃ ᵊn

88

EXERCISE 18
1. Yes, there is an alternative pronunciation of the middle syllable of **exorcise**, giving 'eks ə saɪz.
2. Two British, and two American:
mə 'dʒɒr ət i, mə 'dʒɒr ɪt i‖mə 'dʒɔːr əʇ i, mə 'dʒɑːr əʇ i
3. No.
4. FALSE. There is an alternative pronunciation: ə'priːs i eɪt.
5. TRUE: **acotyledon** ‚eɪ ˌkɒt ɪ⟨liːdᵊn‚ə⟩ˌkɒt-‚⟨æ-,‚ə⟩'‑‑, The alternatives circled can be combined to give ə ˌkɒt ə 'liːd ən.

EXERCISE 19: 1. **reassessment** riː‿ə 'ses mənt   2. **reassigned** ‚riː‿ə 'saɪnd
3. **reassuring** ‚riː‿ə 'ʃɔːr ɪŋ   4. **reawakens** ‚riː‿ə 'weɪk ənz

EXERCISE 20: 1. 'mɑːrk əʇ əd   2. 'kaɪnd li nəs   3. 'juːs ləs li   4. TRUE
5. 'eɪdʒ əns iz

EXERCISE 21

	Main	Alter-native	Reg-ional	AmE	AmE alter-native
3. Aberdaron	‚æb ə'dær ən			‚æb ᵊr'dær ən	‚æb ᵊr'der ən
4. ballroom	'bɔːl ruːm	'bɔːl rʊm	biː 'heɪv		
5. behave	bɪ 'heɪv	bə 'heɪv			
6. economics	‚iːk ə 'nɒm ɪks	‚ek ə 'nɒm ɪks		‚iːk ə 'nɑːm ɪks	‚ek ə 'nɑːm ɪks
7. managing	'mæn ɪdʒ ɪŋ	'mæn ədʒ ɪŋ			
8. target	'tɑːg ɪt		'tɑːg ət	'tɑːrg ət	

EXERCISE 22

	Main	Alter-native	Reg-ional	'In-correct'	AmE	AmE alter-native
3. Buckingham	'bʌk ɪŋ əm		'bʌk ɪŋ həm	bʌk ən əm		
4. dancing	'dɑːnˈs ɪŋ		'dænˈs ɪŋ		'dænˈs ɪŋ	
5. mistake	mɪ 'steɪk	mə 'steɪk				
6. Saturday	'sæt ə deɪ	'sæt ə di		'sæt di	'sæʇ ᵊr deɪ	'sæʇ ᵊr di
7. tariff	'tær ɪf		'tær əf		'ter ɪf	'ter əf
8. trauma	'trɔːm ə	'traʊm ə			'traʊm ə	'trɔːmə 'trɑːmə

EXERCISE 23b

	in full	*with elision*
1. French	frentʃ	frenʃ
2. plunge	plʌndʒ	plʌnʒ
3. stamped	stæmpt	stæmt
4. tangerine	ˌtændʒ ə ˈriːn	tænʒ ə ˈriːn
5. tasteful	ˈteɪst fʊl	ˈteɪs fʊl
6. kindness	ˈkaɪnd nəs	ˈkaɪn nəs
7. awaken	ə ˈweɪk ən	ə ˈweɪk n

EXERCISE 24: 2. E 3. E 4. F 5. F 6. E

EXERCISE 25

	in full	*with elision*
1. pinch	pɪntʃ	pɪnʃ
2. bandstand	ˈbænd stænd	ˈbæn stænd
3. camped	kæmpt	kæmt
4. wistful	ˈwɪst fʊl	ˈwɪs fʊl
5. softness	ˈsɒft nəs	ˈsɒf nəs
6. textbook	ˈtekst bʊk	ˈteks bʊk

EXERCISE 26: softly, lounge, firstly, wasteful

EXERCISE 27: 3. ˈdɪst ənts 4. mɪns 5. ˈtraɪ ʌmpf 6. ə ˈkweɪnt ənts 7. ˈkʌmf ət 8. ˈempf ə sɪs 9. ə ˈsɪst əns 10. səb ˈstæntʃ l

EXERCISE 28
KEY A:

A: I've just had my lounge decorated. It hadn't been done since I moved in.
B: What colour is it?
A: It's called French Blush.
B: Very tasteful, I'm sure, but it doesn't convey anything.
A: Well, on the chart it looked lovely – a sort of pale tangerine colour.
B: That sounds nice. The lounge faces north, doesn't it, and a tangerine glow would take away the coldness.
A: That's just what I thought: elegant but comfortable. But actually it's more like orange. It's cheerful – but not very restful.

KEY B:

A: aɪv dʒʌs hæd maɪ laʊnʒ dek ə reɪt ɪd ‖ ɪt hæd nt biːn dʌn sɪns aɪ muːvd ɪn

B: wɒt kʌl ər ɪz ɪt

A: ɪts kɔːld frenʃ blʌʃ

B: veri teɪst fʊl aɪm ʃɔː ‖ bət ɪt dʌz nt kən veɪ en i θɪŋ

A: wel ɒn ðə tʃɑːt ɪt lʊk lʌv li ‖ ə sɔːt əv peɪl tænʒ ər iːn kʌl ə

B: ðæt saʊndz naɪs ‖ ðə laʊndʒ feɪs ɪz nɔːθ dʌz n ɪt ‖ ənd ə tændʒ ər iːn gləʊ wʊd teɪk ə weɪ ðə kəʊld nəs

A: ðæts dʒʌs wɒt aɪ θɔːt ‖ el ɪ gənt bət kʌmpft əb l ‖ bət æk tʃu əl i ɪts mɔː laɪk ɒr ɪndʒ ‖ ɪts tʃɪə fʊl ‖ bət nɒt veri res fʊl

EXERCISE 29b

	syllabic consonant	*vowel + consonant*
1. **suddenly**	'sʌd n li	'sʌd ən li
2. **Britain**	'brɪt n	'brɪt ən
3. **frightening**	'fraɪt n ɪŋ	'fraɪt ən ɪŋ
4. **hidden**	'hɪd n	'hɪd ən
5. **medal**	'med l	'med əl
6. **needlework**	'niːd l wɜːk	'niːd əl wɜːk
7. **cattle**	'kæt l	'kæt əl
8. **petals**	'pet lz	
9. **panel**	'pæn l	'pæn əl
10. **softener**	'sɒf n e	'sɒf ən ə
11. **station**	'steɪ ʃn	'steɪ ʃən
12. **fastened**	'fɑːs nd	'fɑːs ənd

EXERCISE 30
KEY A

GOLDEN OLDIES – the most popular songs chosen by radio listeners:
The Battle of New Orleans
Wooden Heart
Beautiful Dreamer
I Beg your Pardon (I never promised you a rose garden)
The Tunnel of Love
Sentimental Journey
Suddenly it's Spring
Congratulations

KEY B: 'gəʊld ən, 'tʃəʊz ən, 'lɪs n əz, 'bæt l, 'wʊd ən, 'bjuːt ɪ fəl, 'paːd n, 'gaːd n, 'tʌn əl, ˌsent ɪ 'ment l, 'sʌd n li, kən ˌgrætʃ u 'leɪʃ ənz

EXERCISE 31: 1. 'æb sənt 2. 'bek ən 3. 'kʌr ənt 4. 'saɪk l 5. 'pæm əl ə
6. 'pær ə gən 7. 'sɜːv nt 8. 'sɪm əl ə 9. 'træv l ə 10. 'veɪk ənt

EXERCISE 32: With three syllables: 'bæt l ɪŋ (recommended pronunciation),
and also: 'bæt əl ɪŋ
With two syllables: 'bæt lɪŋ

EXERCISE 33: 3. flattening 2̣. 4. sprinkling 3̣. 5. cycling 3̣.
6. reckoning 2̣. 7. threatening 3̣. 8. trickling 2̣.

EXERCISE 34: 1. 'mæd n ɪŋ 2. 'bæt lɪŋ 3. 'flæt nɪŋ 4. 'sprɪŋk l ɪŋ
5. 'saɪk l ɪŋ 6. 'rek nɪŋ 7. 'θret n ɪŋ 8. 'trɪk lɪŋ

EXERCISE 35

Words with no compression: always three syllables eg. finally 'faɪn ᵊl i	Words with compression: can be two syllables eg. traveller 'træv ᵊl ə
'gləʊb ᵊl i	'keəf li
'nɔ:m əl i	'leŋθ nɪŋ
'sʌm ər aɪz	'nɜ:s ri
'təʊt əl i	'sɑːmp lɪŋ
'tʌn ᵊl ɪŋ	

EXERCISE 36b

	full	with compression
1. obvious 'ɒb vi.əs	'ɒb vi əs	'ɒb vjəs
2. bicentennial ˌbaɪ sen 'ten i.əl	ˌbaɪ sen 'ten i əl	ˌbaɪ sen 'ten jəl
3. studious 'stju:d i.əs	'stju:d i əs	'stju:d jəs
4. usual 'ju:ʒ u.əl	'ju:ʒ u əl	'ju:ʒ wəl
5. material mə 'tɪer i.əl	mə 'tɪər i əl	mə 'tɪər jəl
6. diagram 'daɪ.ə græm	'daɪ ə græm	'daə græm

EXERCISE 37: 3. C 4. F 5. C 6. C 7. F 8. C 9. F

EXERCISE 38
8 words with syllabic consonants: haven't, reputable, rotten, label,
Revolution, celebration, classical, education.
2 words with compression involving a consonant: company, anniversary.
5 words with compression involving vowels: flowered, biennial, biannual,
obviously, bicentennial.

A: ðiːz plɑːnts hæv nt flaəd ət ɔːl ðɪs jɪə‖aɪ bɔːt ðəm frəm ə rep jə təb l
kʌmp ni‖bət aɪ θɪŋk ðeɪ mʌs bi rɒt n
B: ðɪs leɪb l sez ðeə baɪ en jelz
A: səʊ ðeɪ ɔːt tə flaʊ ə twaɪs ə jɪə
B: nəʊ ðəʊz ə baɪ æn julz‖baɪ en jəl plɑːnts əʊn li flaʊ ə ev ri ʌð ə jɪə‖jɔː plɑːnts
ɒb vjəs ly ɑːnt flaʊ ər ɪŋ bɪ kɒz ðɪs ɪs ðə fɜːʃ jɪə
A: aɪ θɔːt ə baɪ en jəl wəz ə sɔːt əv tuː hʌndr əd jɪər æn ɪ vɜːs ri‖naɪn tiːn eɪt i naɪn
wəz ðə baɪ en jəl əv ðə frenʃ rev ə luːʃ n‖ən ðə wəz ə greɪt sel ɪ breɪʃ n ɪn pæ rɪs
B: nəʊ jɔː θɪŋk ɪŋ əv baɪ sen ten jəl
A: əʊ ði əd vɑːnt ɪdʒ ɪz əv ə klæs ɪk l ed ju keɪʃ n

92

EXERCISE 39: 2. es'cort   3. 'survey   4. con'vert   5. 'contest   6. 'insult

EXERCISE 40: <u>contrast</u>, <u>reject</u>, <u>present</u>, <u>transport</u>

EXERCISE 42   KEY A: choose from these words:
content, contract, desert, extract, minute, object, refuse

KEY B: 2. refuse   rɪf 'juːz
                        'ref juːs
3. contract   kən 'trækt
              'kɒn trækt
4. content   kən 'tent
             'kɒn tent
5. extract   ɪk 'strækt
             'ek strækt
6. object   əb 'jekt
            'ɒb jekt
7. minute   maɪ 'njuːt
            'mɪn ɪt
8. desert   dɪ 'zɜːt
            'dez ət

EXERCISE 43: 2. break-in   3. comeback   4. walkout   5. flashback
6. downpour   7. breakdown   8. countdown   9. lift-off   10. outlay

EXERCISE 44: ar'rest   'vagabond   'anyone   i'magining   'notice
dis'parity   be'tween   'accent   'later   dis'covered   'never   'happened
'instantly   'everyone's   de'meanour   a'bruptly   'hawker   'barrow
up'set   be'fore   'noticed   'attitude   'women   'varies   'badly   'shudder
a'way   'movement   dis'gust   'powerful   'difficult   'genuinely
de'graded   ir'rational   'prison

EXERCISE 45: 2. ə 'dʒend ə   3. 'æg rə veɪt   4. 'eɪ dʒənt   5. ə 'gres ɪv
6. 'æg rəʊ   7. ə 'gluːt ɪn ət ɪv   8. 'ædʒ aɪl   9. ə 'grænd ɪz mənt

EXERCISE 46: 1. ˌanniˈversary   2. ˌdefiˈnition   3. ˌepicuˈrean
4. ˌmediˈocrity   5. ˌmetaˈphysical   6. ˌmortifiˈcation   7. ˌproclaˈmation
8. reˌgeneˈration   9. ˌvaleˈdiction

The Metaphysical Poets
A selection of poems

Mediocritie in love rejected	Thomas Carew
A Valediction: forbidding mourning	John Donne
The Anniversarie	John Donne
An Ode upon his Majestie's Proclamation	Sir Richard Fanshawe
An Epicurean Ode	John Hall
Mortification	George Herbert
The Definition of Love	Andrew Marvell
Regeneration	Henry Vaughan

EXERCISE 48: 2. 'octo°syllable 3. re'vision°ism 4. 'care°taker
5. 'casta°way 6. 'under°carriage 7. 'up°bringing 8. ob'struction°ism
9. 'office°holder 10. e'state °agent 11. 'record °library 12. 'Oedipus
°complex 13. un'certainty °principle

EXERCISE 50: 2. ,inter°conti'nental 3. ,sado°maso'chistic
4. ,vale°tudi'narian 5. Re,ceived pro°nunci'ation 6. ,co-ef°ficient of
'friction 7. ,occu°pational 'therapy

EXERCISE 51: 1. ty'rrannicide 2. ,indi°visi'bility 3. ,sacri'ficial
4. 'care°taker 5. 'liberator 6. ,ado'lescence 7. 'sacrosanct
8. ,intel'lectual 9. ,uncon°vention'ality 10. 'capital°ism

EXERCISE 54: 2. a ,large-scale 'map 3. ,open-heart 'surgery
4. a ,laid-back 'personality 5. a , left-handed po'tato-peeler
6. a ,misspelt 'letter 7. a ,misspent 'youth

EXERCISE 55
1a. ,audio-'visual b. ,audio-°visual 'aids
2a. ,auto'matic b. ,auto°matic 'pilot
3a. ,occu'pational b. ,occu°pational 'therapy
4a. ,ope'rational b. ,ope°rational re'search
5a. ,radio'active b. ,radio°active de'cay

EXERCISE 56
(suggested versions: others are possible)
2. the sun at midday
3. an agent who works undercover
4. income which is unearned
5. a man who is middle-aged
6. railings made of cast-iron
7. a kid who is crazy and mixed-up

EXERCISE 59

Early stress eg. 'picture frame	Late stress eg. ,central 'heating
Spanish lessons	Monday evenings
evening classes	English teacher
Community Centre	Spanish accent
study group	civil engineer
driving instructor	driving ambition
grammar book	South America

EXERCISE 60

1a. an 'English ˌteacher   b. an ˌEnglish 'teacher
2a. a 'darkroom   b. a ˌdark 'room
3a. a 'blackboard   b. a ˌblack 'board
4a. a 'glass shelf   b. a ˌglass 'shelf

EXERCISE 61: Late stress: rubber duck, apple pie, cheese sauce, jam sandwich, peach brandy, salt beef
Early stress: rubber plant, apple blossom, cheese grater, jam jar, peach stone, salt cellar

EXERCISE 62
Early stress: – written as one word: 'Knightsbridge, 'Moorgate
             – with street: 'Baker Street, 'Bond Street
Late stress: ˌTower 'Hill, ˌCharing 'Cross, ˌLeicester 'Square, ˌPiccadilly 'Circus, ˌMarble 'Arch, ˌTottenham ˌCourt 'Road, ˌOxford 'Circus

EXERCISE 64b: 1. absolute 'æbs ə luːt⌣ 2. backgammon ⌒bækˌgæm ən⌒'···
3. backpedal ˌbæk'ped l⌣ 4. caviar ⌒kæv i ɑː⌒,···
5. cigarette ⌒sɪg ə 'ret⌒'··· 6. manageress ˌmæn idʒ ə 'res⌒···⌒
7. submarine 'sʌb mə riːn⌒⌣ 8. ⌒Adam's 'apple⌒'··ˌ·· 9. ice'cream ⌒⌣
10. ⌒radio a'larm⌒'···ˌ·

EXERCISE 65c
          Ⓜ/A   M/Ⓐ
1. Is ˌvalue 'added tax charged on 'video-casˌsettes?
          Ⓜ/A   M/Ⓐ
2. My neighbour is a ˌvio'linist. She plays a 'violin made in the
   M/Ⓐ
   ˌVirgin 'Islands.

3. Old leather books can be preserved by treating the surface
      Ⓜ/A   Ⓜ/A
   with 'vaseline, and wrapping them in ˌvelve'teen.

          Ⓜ/A
4. I was once offered a job doing a 'voiceˌover for a television
   advertisement. The pay was marvellous, but I developed an
          M/Ⓐ
   infection of the 'vocal cords and couldn't do it.

5. 'Who said that the only meaningful statements are those which are
      M/Ⓐ   Ⓜ/A
   ˌveri'fiable by sense experience?' 'It sounds like ˌVol'taire.'

EXERCISE 66c

2. applicable   ə 'plɪk əb l   M
3. primarily   praɪ 'mer əl i   A
4. subsidence   səb 'saɪd ns   M
5. decade   dɪ 'keɪd   A
6. communal   'kɒm jʊn l   M
7. harass   'hær əs   M
8. controversy   kən 'trɒv əs i   A
9. clandestine   klæn 'dest ɪn   M
10. contributed   kən 'trɪb jut ɪd   M

EXERCISE 67

a. 2. in'form ,infor'mation   Yes
   3. ,enter'tain ,enter'tainment   No
   4. e'lectric e,lec'tricity   Yes
   5. 'careless 'carelessness   No
b. 1. 'plenty 'plentiful   No
   2. 'photograph ,photo'graphic   Yes
   3. 'beauty 'beautiful   No
   4. 'value 'valuable   No
   5. Ja'pan ,Japa'nese   Yes

EXERCISE 68

a.   'launder   ,launde'rette   3. S
   B. 'comfort   'comfortable   1. SN
      'period   ,peri'odical   2. SI

      'punctual   ,punctu'ality   2. SI
   C. wide   'widen   1. SN
      'mountain   ,mountai'neer   3. S

      ci'gar   ,ciga'rette   3. S
   D. e'conomy   ,eco'nomic   2. SI
      'sympathy   'sympathise   1. SN

      'punish   'punishment   1. SN
   E. 'picture   ,pictu'resque   3. S
      'proverb   pro'verbial   2. SI

b.

Stress-neutral	Stress-imposing	Stressed
-ous	-ic	-ese
-able	-ical	-ette
-en	-ity	-eer
-ise	-ial	-esque
-ment		

EXERCISE 70: 1. stɜˤ 2. θɜˤːd 3. 'liːd r 4. 'lɑːrdʒ r 5. bɑːrn

EXERCISE 71: 1. kræft 2. flæsk 3. 'læft r 4. bə'næn ə 5. pæst

EXERCISE 72

RP 1. ɒ wrong   GenAm 4. ɑː card, wrong, harm
    2. ɔː cord, lawn, thorn   5. ɒː lawn
    3. ɑː card, harm   6. ɔː cord, thorn

EXERCISE 73

     ɪ   ə   a   ə   ə   ə
1. cabbage 2. robin 3. habit 4. panic 5. Lenin 6. wicked

    ɪ   ə   ɪ
7. vanish 8. arches 9. carriage

EXERCISE 74

a.   RP   GenAm
   1. **staring**   'steər ɪŋ   'ster ɪŋ
   2. **careful**   'keəf l   'kerf l
   3. **dearest**   'dɪər ɪst   'dɪr ɪst
   4. **experience** ɪk 'spɪər i əns ɪk 'spɪr i əns
   5. **variation**   ,veər i 'eɪʃ n ,ver i 'eɪʃ n
   6. **sincerely**   sɪn 'sɪə li   sɪn 'sɪr li

b.   RP   GenAm
   1. **staring**   'steər ɪŋ   'ster ɪŋ
   2. **careful**   'keəf l   'kerf l
   3. **dearest**   'dɪər ɪst   'dɪr ɪst
   4. **experience** ɪk 'spɪər i əns ɪk 'spɪr i əns
   5. **variation**   ,veər i 'eɪʃ n ,ver i 'eɪʃ n
   6. **sincerely**   sɪn 'sɪə li   sɪn 'sɪr li

EXERCISE 75

1. writing 2. later 3. return 4. related 5. softer 6. attic 7. attack
8. lightning
t is not voiced in 'return' and 'attack' because the t is not at the end of a
syllable.
t is not voiced in 'softer' and 'lightning' because the t is not between
vowels.

EXERCISE 76

1. (rafter) rather rock rod
2. after class (father) ghastly
3. sordid (worthy) warden warm

EXERCISE 77

RP rhymes		GenAm rhymes	
nought	court	bother	father
clerk	mark	abbot	habit
laugh	scarf	sorry	story

EXERCISE 78

ðə 'kɑːr|wəz ə 'dɑːrk 'bluː|'sev n 'pæs ndʒ r|sɪ 'dæn‖ə 'pæk rd|əv ðə 'leɪʈ əs
'mɑːd l|'kʌst əm 'bɪlt‖ɪt wəz ðə 'kaɪnd əv 'kɑːr|jə 'wer jə 'roʊp 'p   lz ɪn‖ɪt wəz
'pɑːrkt|baɪ ə 'faɪr ₒhaɪdr ənt|ən ə 'dɑːrk|'fɔːr ən 'lʊk ɪŋ ʃoʊ 'f |wəð ə 'feɪs əv
'kɑːrvd 'wʊd|wəz bɪ 'haɪnd ðə 'hwiːl‖ði ɪn 'tɪr i r|wəz ə 'poʊlst rd|ɪn 'kwɪlt əd 'greɪ
ʃə 'niːl‖ði 'ɪnd i ən|'pʊt mi ən ðə 'bæk‖'sɪʈ ɪŋ ðer ə 'loʊn|aɪ 'felt|laɪk ə 'haɪ klæs
'kɔːrps‖ 'leɪd 'aʊt|baɪ ən 'ʌnd r teɪk r|wəð ə 'lɑːʈ əv 'gʊd 'teɪst‖

ði 'ɪnd i ən|'gɑːʈ 'ɪn|bɪ 'saɪd ðə ʃoʊ 'f |ən ðə 'kɑːr 't   nd|ɪn ðə 'mɪd l əv ðə
'blɑːk|ən ə 'kɑːp ə 'krɒːs ðə 'striːt|sed 'heɪ|'wiːk li|əz 'ɪf i 'dɪd n 'miːn ət|ən
'ðen|'bent 'daʊn 'kwɪk li|tə 'taɪ ɪʒ 'ʃuː‖

wi 'went 'west|'drɑːpt 'oʊv r tə 'sʌn set|ən slɪd 'fæst ən 'nɔɪz ləs|ə 'lɒːŋ 'ðæt‖ði
'ɪnd i ən 'sæt 'moʊʃ n ləs|bɪ 'saɪd ðə ʃoʊ 'f   ‖ən ə 'keɪʒ nəl 'hwɪʃ|əv hɪz
'p   s n 'æl ət i|'drɪft əd 'bæk tə mi‖ðə 'draɪv r|'lʊkt əz əf hi wəz 'hæf ə 'sliːp|bəʈ i
'pæst ðə 'fæst bɔɪz|ɪn ðə kən'v   ʈ əb l sɪ 'dænz|əz 'ðoʊ ðeɪ wr 'biː ɪŋ 'toʊd‖ðeɪ
'tɜᵛːnd 'ɑːn|'ɒːl ðə 'griːn 'laɪts fɔːr ɪm‖'sʌm 'draɪv rz r 'laɪk ðæt‖hiː 'nev r 'mɪst
'hwʌn‖

ɪʈ əd bɪn ə 'wɔːrm 'æft r 'nuːn|bət ðə 'hiːt wəz 'gɒːn‖wiː 'hwɪpt pæst ə 'dɪst ənt
'klʌst r|əv 'laɪʈ əd 'bɪld ɪŋz|ənd ən 'end ləs 'sɪr iːz əv 'laɪʈ əd 'mænʃ nz|'nɑːt tuː
'kloʊs tə ðə 'roʊd‖wiː 'dɪpt 'daʊn|tə 'sk   ʈ ə 'hjuːdʒ 'griːn 'poʊl oʊ fiːld|wɪθ ə
'nʌð r|'iːk wəl i 'hjuːdʒ 'prækt əs fiːld|bə 'saɪd ɪt|'sɔːrd ə gen tə ðə 'tɑːp əv ə 'hɪl|ən
'swʌŋ 'maʊnt n wrd|ʌp ə 'stiːp 'hɪl 'roʊd|əv 'kliːn 'kɑːn kriːt|ðət 'pæst 'ɔːr ndʒ
groʊvz|sʌm 'rɪtʃ mænz 'pet|bɪ kəz ðɪs əz 'nɑːt 'ɔːr ndʒ 'kʌntr i‖ən ðen 'lɪʈ l baɪ
'lɪʈ l|ðə 'laɪʈ əd 'wɪnd oʊz|əv ðə 'mɪl jə 'nerz hoʊmz|wr 'gɒːn|ən ðə 'roʊd
'nær oʊd|ən 'ðɪs|wəz 'stɪl wʊd 'haɪts‖

EXERCISE 79: 2. D 3. S 4. S 5. D 6. S 7. D 8. D 9. S 10. S

EXERCISE 80

	Acronym	Separate letters
3. Organisation for Economic Co-operation and Development		OECD
4. Organisation of Petroleum Exporting Countries	OPEC 'əʊp ek	
5. Trades Union Congress		TUC
6. Universities Central Council on Admissions	UCCA 'ʌk ə	
7. University of California at Los Angeles.		UCLA
8. unilateral declaration of independence		UDI
9. United Nations Educational, Scientific and Cultural Organisation	UNESCO ju 'nesk əʊ	

EXERCISE 82: 1. 'kræm bər‿i 2. ʌm 'bæl əns 3. 'ɪm pʊt 4. ʌŋ 'greɪt fᵊl 5. 'rek ɔːb ˌbreɪk ə/z 6. 'mɪb pɔɪnt 7. 'brɔːg kɑːst 8. 'wiːg ˌkɪl ə

EXERCISE 83: 1. 'kɒs tʃuːm 2. tjuːb 3. 'mɪl dju: 4. ə 'dʒuːs 5. 'æmpl ɪ tʃuːd 6. rɪ 'djuːs 7. ˌedʒ u 'keɪʃ n 8. riː 'kɒnst ɪ tjuːt

EXERCISE 84

hi swʌŋ raʊn stɑːtld‖ə nɒk ɒn ɪz dɔː‖ðeə mʌs bi sʌm mɪsteɪk‖ɔːr ɪz ɪəz wə pleɪɪŋ ɪm trɪks‖ðə dɑːknəs əv ðə rʊm|fər i əd nɒtʃet swɪtʃt ɒn ðə laɪts|meɪd ðɪs siːm mɔː plɔːzəbl‖bət nəʊ‖ðə nɒk wəz rɪpiːtɪd ‖kʌm ɪn|hi sed ɪn ə θɪŋ krækt vɔɪs| əŋ klɪəd ɪz θrəʊt‖kʌm ɪn‖hi muːvd iːgəli təwɔːdz ðə dɔː|tə welkəm ɪz vɪzɪtə|ən tə tɜːn ðə laɪts ɒn ət ðə seim taɪm‡bək kəlaɪdɪd wɪð ə tʃeə|ən dropt ɪz sɪgɑː| wɪtʃ rəʊld ʌndə ðə teɪbl ‖ hi daɪvd ɑːftər ɪt əz ðə dɔːr əʊpənd‖ə segmənt əv laɪt frəm ðə kɒrɪdɔː fel əkrɒs ðə flɔː|bət dɪd nɒt rɪviːl ðə haɪdɪŋ pleɪs əv ðə sɪgɑː‖ə wʊmənz vɔɪs sed ʌnsɜːtnli|prəfesə zæp‖

jeə|kʌm ɪn‖wʊdʒuː swɪtʃ ðə laɪt ɒn pliːz‖

ðə laɪts keɪm ɒn|ən i hɜːd ðə wʊmən gɑːsp‖weər ɑː juː‖

ʌndə hɪə‖hi faʊnd ɪmself steərɪŋ ət ə peər əv θɪk fɜː laɪmb buːts|ən ðə hemlaɪn əv ə ʃægi fɜː kəʊt‖tə ðiːz wəz ædɪd|ə məʊmənt leɪtə|ən invɜːtɪd fiːmeɪl feɪs| skɑːvd|red nəʊzd|ən æprɪhensɪv‖

aɪl bi raɪt wɪð ju|hi sed‖aɪ drɒpt maɪ sɪgɑː sʌmweər ʌndə hɪə‖

EXERCISE 85

refinement rɪ 'faɪm mənt
Anticipatory dealveolar assimilation of the n, anticipating the m.

patrol pə 'trɒul
Use of special allophone ɒʊ before l in the same syllable.

tempestuous tem 'peʃ tʃu̯əs
Assimilation of the s, anticipating the following tʃ.

cardboard 'kɑːb bɔːd
Anticipatory dealveolar assimilation of the d, anticipating the b.

institution ˌɪnˈst ɪ 'tʃuːʃ ᵊn
Assimilation: coalescence of t and j to form tʃ.

handgun 'hæŋ gʌn
Elision of d, plus assimilation of n, anticipiating the g.

enfold ɪn 'fɒʊld
Use of special allophone ɒʊ before l in the same syllable.

Wibsey 'wɪp si
Assimilation: the b is devoiced, anticipating the following unvoiced s.

tune tʃuːn
Assimilation: coalescence of t and j to form tʃ.

landmark 'læm mɑːk
Elision of d, plus assimilation of n, anticipating the m.

EXERCISE 86

b.
sev rəl lʌn dən peɪp əz kleɪmd tə deɪ ðət ə bɜːg əl ri həd teɪk n pleɪs ət bʌk ɪŋ həm pæl ɪs‖ə spəʊks pɜːs n rɪf juːzd tə kɒn fɑːm weð ər ɔː nɒt eni θɪŋk əd biːn stəʊl ən‖ə njuːk jəl ə paʊ ə steɪʃ n ɪn bæŋ ə|nɔːθ weɪlz|həz biːn kləʊʒd daʊn|waɪl meɪn teɪn əns wɜːk ɪz kær id aʊt‖æʃ felt ɒn ðe ruːf əv ðə meɪn ri æk tə bɪldɪŋ həz krækt|ənd ə kjuːm ə leɪt ɪd deb ri niːdz tə biː ri muːvd‖ə ləʊk l preʃ ə gruːp kleɪm ðət ɪŋ kriːst ɪn sɪd əns əv maɪ greɪn ɪn ði eər i ə|hz djuː tə reɪd i eɪʃ ɪ skeɪp ɪŋ θruː ðə kræks‖ðə mæn ɪdʒ mənt əv ðə plɑːnt dɪnaɪ ðɪs əz ə mɪs tʃiːv əs ə tempt tə kɔːz ə lɑːm‖ənd naʊ hɪər ɪz ðə leɪt ɪst weðə fɔː kɑːst frəm ðə miːt ər ə lɒdʒ ɪk l ɒf ɪs

c.

Word	Pronunciation on cassette	Alternative, regional or 'incorrect'?	Recommended pronunciation
Buckingham	'bʌk ɪŋ həm	regional	'bʌk ɪŋ əm
confirm	kɒn 'fɜːm	regional	kən 'fɜːm
anything	'en i θɪŋk	incorrect	'en i θɪŋ
nuclear	'njuːk jəl ə	incorrect	'njuːk li ə
Bangor	'bæŋ ə	incorrect	'bæŋ gə
maintenance	meɪn 'teɪn əns	incorrect	'meɪn tən əns
asphalt	'æʃ felt	incorrect	'æs fælt
accumulated	ə 'kjuːm ə leɪt ɪd	incorrect	ə 'kjuːm jə leɪt ɪd
migraine	'maɪ greɪn	alternative	'miː greɪn
mischievous	mɪs 'tʃiːv əs	incorrect	'mɪs tʃɪv əs
Meteorological	ˌmiːt ər ə 'lɒdʒ ɪk l	incorrect	ˌmiːt i ər ə 'lɒdʒ ɪk l